Real Estate Grind

The Inner City's

Goldmine

by

Khalfani A. Ajamu

Paperback: ISBN 978-0-578-29464-3
Hardcover: ISBN 979-8-218-13266-8

Paper Over Pauper Publishing
New Haven ~ Connecticut

Real Estate Grind

The Inner City's

Goldmine

Table of Contents

In loving memory of my mother Linda Bowers, My father Donald Brown, my maternal grandmother Anna Bowers and My uncle, Glen Normon Bowers, my aunt The Evangelist Beatrice Rawls, my grandfather Roger Bowers and a host of other relatives! All of you have impacted my life in so many different ways, and I cherish in my heart the moments I was blessed to share with you. You are all deeply loved and truly missed!!

Special thanks and recognition to my dear aunt Evangelist Beatrice Rawls (Aunt Bea Bea) who sowed a spiritual seed into my natural life while I was still in my infancy stages of life. Knowing that the fruit of her belief in that seed would someday come to pass. I love you for that auntie.

To my children and remaining immediate family members (especially my grandchildren), know that you are loved and cared about immensely!

A heartfelt thanks to my many mentors along my life journey. Your bountiful wisdom shared with me as you can see was not in vain! I am truly grateful for the time and commitment you put into making sure that I reach my full potential. As a sponge I absorbed it all, but just like a sponge, I can only absorb so much before it must be given back. I too, now find myself at the point in life where I must give back!

Foreword

Let me state from the outset that this is not a book that is fluff filled. It is a financial, informational, self-development, motivational based one. It is written for both male and females, old and young. It has been written to transcend the constraints of geography. If you're black, white, Latino, and you reside in the inner city anywhere in America, then this book is exclusively for you. This isn't a get rich quick book either. As the title states it's a Grind, and Your attitude about this particular grind will determine Your financial altitude as a partaker of this grind! This grind can be recession proof when executed properly. (i.e., you will be fine even when the overall economy is doing bad). In this book, I will present ways you can explore, to tap into this Goldmine Reservoir that is right at your fingertips.

What encouraged me to write this book was the growing concern I have regarding the economic plight of my inner-city brothers and sisters, as well as the geographic and social conditions they have been accepting for far too long! Although this book is not exhaustive, its contents are meant to be informative, comprehensive, and ultimately galvanizing, (stimulating) to the reader. The kind is stimulation that produces action!

As it relates to the inner-city areas of society, historically there has been a lack of real estate investment interest on the part of those that reside within the community, and those who live outside of the community. But now there seems to be an overwhelming interest and growing trend by outsiders now investing in the inner cities! Have you ever asked why? I will tell you why. It is because they have access to information that makes properties in the inner city's goldmines, in spite of appearing rundown, boarded up and in some cases vacant.

In a lot of instances, this is why you see that the person collecting the rent looks nothing like its occupants. It's time to change all of this! This book is designed to empower the reader (you) with the information that will enrich your cognitive skills (mental ability) as it relates to real estate investing and create a desire in you to change your socioeconomic and geographic reality, and consequently change the quality of life for your family, and the environment in which you live.

Throughout this book, you will notice that I have consciously stayed away from the term "Ghetto" to describe these areas. Why? Because when you get into the etymology of the word, (the word's origin) Ghettos were not created for you. Let's take a look at the Webster's Collegiate dictionary to reference the word ghetto.

Ghetto (formerly in most European countries) a section of a city in which all Jews were required to live. 2. A section predominantly inhabited by Jews. [1605-15] <It's Origin>. The name of an Island near Venice where Jews were forced to reside in the 16th century.

Ghetto is a noun and is derived from the word Get Tare (which means to throw).

So based on its origin, the term ghetto (and the definition associated with it) should not be applied to the environment where you currently reside. Since then though the Jewish community has made a conscious, concerted effort, to make sure that they will never again allow anyone to relegate them to a life of servitude, or that of a pauper! Kudos to them for maintaining the resolution it required to overcome the challenges they were faced with and establish themselves as a dynamic collective (people committed to working together), who also have used the power of real estate investing to achieve wealth!

In fact, if you were able to look at the investment portfolio of all the wealthy families in the United States and abroad, you will notice that the common link they all share is real estate investment!

Now let's look at its contemporary meaning.

Ghetto- a section of a City, especially a thickly populated Slum area, inhabited predominantly by members of an Ethnic or other Minority group, often as a result of the ***Social*** *or* ***Economic*** *restrictions, pressures or hardships.*

I hope you have noticed the words Social and Economic are in the bold print. You have some in society that will have you to believe that your current environmental standings are exclusively a socioeconomic issue. This is only the byproduct of a more deeply entrenched issue, and that is lack of know-how, and the resolve to apply it when necessary!

You see they are already in the know. While on the other hand, not making this information readily known to you. Most people that invest in the urban communities are privy to and are effectively utilizing the information in this book to their benefit but will not enlighten you on the accessibility of this information because of their predisposition that you will become their competition. Which goes to show you that some people in life will find you tolerable and even likable, as long as you remain in a non-threatening position to their interest or in this case Goldmine.

This is the focal point of the book, to provide you with insight as to why The Real Estate Grind is the Inner Cities Gold mine! As I write the foreword to this book, I am reminded of the children of Israel who did not know that their physical Exodus from Egypt (Bondage) would come by way of Moses (God appointed one) who grew up in their midst. And you the reader will be surprised to learn from this book, that your financial exodus (out of social economic bondage) has always been amongst you as well.

The information contained in this book is to introduce you to The Property Equity Niche Investment Approach. The word "Niche" means a place, employment, or activity (in this instance real estate investing) for which a person or thing is best fitted. (Also taken from the Webster Collegiate Dictionary). This book is based on real estate investment, but the Niche is investing in run down properties, located in the inner-city areas. Familiar territory to you if you reside there. In this book I will provide you with information on HUD (Department of Housing and Urban Development) related programs and grant programs created to assist those that are willing to invest in the areas zoned for housing financial assistance. Again, this book listed resources are not exhaustive, but it does introduce you to some of the programs that are out there. I will provide you with ideas on who your investment team should consist of, how to raise private capital through partnerships, and how the Community Reinvestment Act can benefit you, and how you can hold your property once purchased.

In some of the chapters you will notice a dichotomy (a two-part section of information) on a Particular subject matter, and also a section titled Author's Thoughts, where I elaborate on the content of the chapter. In my opinion, multifamily property investment should come before single-family home ownership. And if you're already in a home in the inner city, seek to buy some of the blighted property that's around you and rent it out.

The outreach effort on my part through this book is to help you realize the latent (hidden potential) you possess, so you can channel it in a way that will enable you to take care of your family, retire with financial stability. and remain out of the United States of America's prison / jail system!

Having stated that, the information in this book is to empower the self-motivator, the one who is sick and tired of being sick and tired, the one who desires to experience the fruits of entrepreneurship. The one who is endeavoring to extricate (free) themselves from the stronghold of an unproductive lifestyle, and the one who thinks that because they don't have a formal education their chances of being successful in real estate is not realistic! And most of all, it's for all those who have allowed the media reports to influence them into thinking that the housing market (especially in the inner cities) is bad right now.

After reading this book your response when you hear that statement again should be "real estate is bad for whom right now? You know perceived hopelessness; lack of knowledge and vision can sometimes be blinding to the point where an individual cannot see the positive avenue of possibilities and probabilities that surrounds them. And unless they're presented with something that represents a ray of hope, they will find themselves entangled by a life of complacency and inertia (inactivity). I pray that this book will serve as that ray of economic hope for you! While living in New Haven, Connecticut in a section of town called Newhallville (the Ville). I can remember seeing abandoned, boarded up houses, not only there but in other areas of town as well. This unacceptable sight became deeply rooted into the social and psychological fabric of my mind as a youth.

Back then, people of African descent thoroughly populated the area I lived in, so it aroused suspicion to see a Caucasian man come into our residential area. Because for the most part, if they came into our area during these times, they were either a drug addict, policeman, (undercover), a delivery man, lost or coming to collect their rent (for the exceptional ones that did decide to invest in the inner city). In retrospect, I can now see that even those select few (outside investors) saw the wisdom in investing there. To them, each vacant, boarded up, and run-down property represented Gold that needed to be mined! And I'm now fully persuaded that their decision to invest in the inner city was predicated on the information that this book provides you with!

You are going to be quite surprised at the housing programs available through the Department of Housing and Urban Development (with Federal funds) for the area you live in. And I'm sure they have plenty more that I'm not aware of but it's a good starting point!

Each state or city has its own Department of Housing and Urban Development Department, who are responsible for creating the housing programs that make affordable housing available to those who need it, and the money available for those who are willing to participate as a developer, investor or landlord.

"Knowledge is Power but only when APTLY applied". Please remember that!

There is an old adage that says, "There are three types of people in life, those that make things happen, those that watch things happen, and Those that stand around and wonder what happened." Who do you choose to be?

Best wishes in your Gold Mind Quest!

Khalfani A. Ajamu.

Ponder These Facts

- Did you know that in the last decade foreign investors have purchased over $100 billion in US inner-city real estate, pricing out locals and displacing longtime residents? It's time to take back our communities!
- Every year government backed gentrification projects displaced thousands of low-income families. But what if we as community members could reclaim our neighborhoods

- One growing up in New Haven, I watched as my community was ravaged by outside investors and government neglect. Now I'm fighting back!
- As a long-life resident of New Haven Connecticut, I've seen the devastating impact of gentrification. That's why I'm dedicated to empowering our community to take control.
- From redlining to blockbusting, the history of inner-city real estate is marked by exploitation, but today we have the power to rewrite that narrative.

- The legacy of urban renewal has left deep scars now it's time for community led renewal.
- Join the movement to reclaim our inner cities invest develop and thrive in the communities you love.

- It's time to stop complaining about gentrification and start building our own community wealth.
- The future of our inner cities is not in the hands of outsiders, but in the hearts of those who call them home.

- Community development without community control is just colonization by another name!

1 Location! Location! Location!

A six-step systematic approach to becoming a property equity niche investor.

Before we begin let's take a look at the article below and see what a housing authority official in the Chicago area had to say about Section-8[1] money in the *Chicago Tribune's* article, "2 lucrative deals for ex-DuPage housing officials? (*see figure 1*).

Location! Location! Location! I can hear that conventional chant even now as I am writing this book. Typically, we are taught to invest in areas where the real estate appreciates in value since the person cannot be talking about the urban communities because in reality as well as historically, properties in the economically oppressed zones are rarely if at all appreciated in value. Because there is never an exorbitant excessive amount of people wanting to live in these as they out aching infested and crime ___ burdened areas.

TRIBUNE WATCHDOG

2 lucrative deals for ex-DuPage housing official

Real estate developer and big political campaign donor Michael Pizzuto received two no-bid contracts to build affordable housing from his former colleagues on the county housing authority board, a Tribune investigation revealed. Said one housing authority official: "That Section 8 money is like gold. That's 20 years of guaranteed monthly payments coming to your property. Everybody wants that." Tribune reporter Bill Ruthhart reports on PAGE 5

Figure Chicago Tribune Article

So, the real estate investment dynamics that govern the

[1] The Housing Choice Vouchers Program, also known as Section 8, provides assistance to eligible low- and moderate-income families to rent housing anywhere, not just in subsidized housing projects. The federal assistance program works as a rental subsidy that allows families to pay a reasonable amount of their income toward rent. https://www.affordablehousing.com/what-is-section8.aspx

middle- and upper-class areas cannot be applied to the inner cities. It has its own character independent of these more (high-end/wealthy) sections. This is one of the reasons why up to this date there hasn't been a book written (that I know of) exclusively for the urban dweller and about the Gold Mine that lies right in your backyard. Those that typically author real estate investment books don't for the most part invest in these areas. Even for those exceptions that do, they don't deem the housing market in these areas economically viable from a national housing platform perspective. The other reason why a book like this has never been written is because those that are in the know will never be inclined to write a book on this subject and reveal all the industry secrets. They tell you just enough to pique your interest and keep you engaged.

Their disillusionment is that you will become a direct threat to their gold mine acquisition monopoly. Should you learn about the real estate grind and all that it has to offer. I, on the other hand, know that it's my divine and civil obligation to make sure that you as well, be able to mine in the same place as the exceptional miners of the gold. In this book the information provided, and the instruction given is not to steer you down the path of appreciation investing (ie, to invest in hopes that the property will go up in value.) The purpose of this book is to clearly show you that the best location for you to invest in is where you rest your hand every night!

Remember in the forward section, I spoke about writing this book on the Property Equity Niche Investment Approach? Well location will be the primary component in <u>your</u> niche investment plan, because the properties that you are targeting are located where? In the inner city. So, location for you in your niche investing is different from the conventional usage of the word location, location, location. When they speak about location, location, location they are saying invest in areas that are not drug infested, crime laden and where the property values appreciate (increase). I have spoken with countless people over the years in the real estate field and believe me they represent the ones that don't have any desire to invest in the urban community.

As a matter of fact, the first thing they usually say is "section eight tenants will tear your property up." And besides, the property doesn't appreciate in value. I laugh and say "those individuals you are talking about are a small percentage.

, The vast majority of section eight tenants will take care of your property as long as you are not a slumlord! They feel that the headaches they could potentially have to deal with, outweighs the strong cash flow that the rent will produce. Remember this information when you become a landlord. Always treat people the way you would like for them to treat you. The urban communities are replete with gold mines (i.e. abandoned buildings). These properties are investment opportunities for you waiting to be realized. All you need is the knowledge, understanding, vision, ambition, commitment and capitol, all essential tools that this book covers.

Investing in economically distressed areas is a very unpopular stance for the typical investor. Which presents the opportunity for you the reader to flourish unlimitedly. Just know that after reading this book the only responsibility is on you is to act. You can't use that tired excuse "I didn't know." And the best part of this investment system is you can move at your own pace. You can be a part time operator or full-time operator. You can purchase your first property and rent it out and be content with that. Or you can employ a more aggressive approach. Again, the choice is yours. You may be thinking, "I'm not really interested in investing in real estate. Fine. But think about it this way. You can use the cash flow from the rent to bank roll or finance whatever your primary field of interest is.

Investing in real estate can be a means to an end. You may say Khalfani, pronounced (Kal-fah-nee). I am not good at math. We'll guess what? I am no mathematician either. But if you understand basic mathematics (i.e., addition, subtraction, multiplication, and division) trust me, you'll do just fine. It's really all about knowing when to combine the different mathematical operations. Since this book has been composed to educate you and not confuse or frustrate you, the real estate formulas that professionals use are not necessarily in this case. Besides they purchase financial calculators with the keys to do the number crunching for them. And nowadays they have software to assist you in crunching the numbers as it pertains to real estate investing.

All you are going to need is a simple calculator starting off. When I think about all those unsuspecting people that invest for appreciation (Which is speculation at best) all because they were lead to believe that if they invested in certain areas, middle class and upper class areas, once the property value increased they could either resell the property at a higher price or grab some of their equity out of the house through a loan process called cash out equity refinancing. Which means that they take out a loan on their equity in the property, which allows the owner of the property to walk away from the loan closing with a check for a certain dollar amount.

This book is designed to safeguard you from the hidden subtle housing manipulation that takes place in the very same areas (middle class and upper-class areas) they encourage you to invest in. My suggestion to you is to operate in the territory you are familiar with (the urban community) until you become highly skilled at recognizing real estate investment opportunities outside of your targeted market!!

So now that you have a better understanding of what the term location, location, location means in a conventional way. Versus what the term should mean to you, you should not be the least bit dismayed, discouraged when you watch CNN, CNBC, the local news or any other coverage on the housing market that says the housing market is bad. As I stated in the foreword, when you hear that statement, your response to yourself should be "bad for whom". Stop looking at life through someone else's lens and start looking at your reality from an analytical informed viewpoint. The best location for you is your location. Remember that!

Author thoughts: To be trained as a real estate investor makes you superficial and robotic minded in your investment approach when qualifying and valuing property for purchase. A lot of conventional real estate investors will purchase property devoid of understanding as it pertains to the potential dangers of investing in real estate for the purpose of appreciation. They are trained, not educated, to find the best locations and purchase the available properties in these areas. Thus, creating an artificial housing value bubble. But to be educated in the real estate investment field makes one more analytical, critical and systematic in the way they operate. It helps you to identify investment opportunities and to safeguard yourself from capital investment losses. You can operate inside of the box or outside of it depending on the circumstances. Too many real estate investors today are being trained and not educated. That's why it will literally pay to be a Property Equity Niche Investor in the inner cities.

2 Operating as a Property Equity Niche Investor

What does the term Property Equity Niche Investment Approach mean? Well, its origin is my real estate modus operation (method of operation) concept. It's what makes me less at risk from the housing market artificial bubbles (in the middle- and upper-class neighborhoods) and more securely positioned to profit in the urban community where I invest in. If you were to meet someone and they asked you "What do you do for a living?" and you responded by saying I am a Property Equity Investor, they would say what's that? And the reason why is that the word equity is typically used in two ways. When describing the amount of value, you have in your property minus the debt owed on it, and also when a company issues stocks (AKA equities).

If you said that you're an equity investor they could possibly think that you are a stock investment. So, when describing the type of real estate investor, you are, it's important to prefix the word equity with the word property, changing it to a title, "Property Equity Niche Investor," rather than a standalone word. The niche target market is that you only buy physically distressed properties in the urban community. But back to what the title Property Equity Niche Investor means. It simply means that you purchase property way below its As Repaired fair market value so that you can establish a profitable equity position upon ownership of the property. This is the reasoning behind purchasing physical distressed properties in the urban communities. This kind of investment is a strict discipline that must be adhered to in order to keep the safeguard protection on yourself needed, and also allow you to reap a huge financial return on your initial invested dollars. Remember the essence of this book is the Real Estate Grind, The Inner City's Gold Mine.

It's about a grind in the inner city. And just like any other grind you have to approach this one systematically (i.e., slow steady and methodically). Being fully committed! This is why I dedicated an entire book to the purchasing of properties within the inner cities exclusively for those that reside in these areas. I realize that once the residents in these areas are empowered with the information contained in this book, they can then apply the investment principles of this grind, and subsequently live a life of financial stability.

As a Property Equity Niche Investor, you must have foresight (the ability to see beyond the current state of the property). And the reason why I say this is because when I was young and growing up in the inner-city, I couldn't see the opportunity when looking at the abandoned and vacant properties, period. What knowledge and foresight does is enable you to look past what's before your eyes and see the end product? Because that's where the Gold lies. Short sightedness has crippled a great many people throughout history and hindered them from evolving into that dynamic individual they were created to be. And that's just what I have set out to accomplish in this book. To help you develop your eye for identifying where (in this case) the Gold lies and provide you with the means to acquire it. And just to reinforce this concept of what Property Equity Niche Investing is, the following illustrations are for the benefit of giving you a clear understanding of what the process requires.

Previously I stated that a Property Equity Niche Investor purchases property way below market values. (Valuation will be discussed in chapter 25). And right now, I want to expound (explain) on that concept a little bit more. By purchasing investment property at a very steep discount, you give yourself a couple of options. One, you can once you own the property borrow against the equity in it, providing that the property is producing income through rents (meaning tenants are renting out your property). Because as a matter of practice a lender will not loan you money on your property as equity until he can determine that you are receiving enough in rents to satisfy your personal bills and your debt service (the monthly mortgage payments you have to make every month).

If you can meet those and other lending requirements the advantage, is you will be able to borrow against the equity in your property tax free (yeah that's right tax free). Remember it's your equity in your property you're borrowing against, so there is no tax liability. But make sure you receive a low fixed rate. This approach is the more favorable amongst investors because it allows you to receive a lump sum of money from your property's equity, and still receive a monthly cash flow from the rents that your tenant pays. This method also enables you to invest in more properties. Since this book is for the entry level investors in the real estate field. I will not proceed any further with this scenario. However, this issue will be covered a little more in another chapter.

Take notice that you are going to purchase property in a distressed condition, so that the return on your initial investment will be quite rewarding. There are two requirements that must be complied with in order for this investment system to be effective. One, you must be willing to follow through on all six steps that make up the system niche approach. And two, the properties you purchase must be two to four families. Caution: if you purchase a single-family home using the property equity niche investor approach your property probably will not produce enough rental income if you rented it out to satisfy a lender's lending requirements or meet your bottom line as an investor. If you find yourself in this type of situation look into converting the single family to a single room occupancy (covered in chapter 16). Other than that, it does not fit into the Property Equity Niche Investment System I will be teaching you about in this book.

So, by comparison, let's look at the differences between how the Property Equity Niche Investor operates, versus the way the conventional property investor operates. Typically, the conventional property investors will not even consider investing in the urban community for various reasons: The property values in the inner cities don't increase at a rate consistent with their property investment appreciation philosophy. These investors generally invest in areas where the property value appreciation is constant. If they do buy a property for less than what it is worth, they will use the fair market value as a starting point and purchase the property for 20 to 30 percent below the fair market value. The properties are typically in habitable condition (meaning fit to rent out). They will use borrowed money either through a lender, an investment partnership or use cash to buy the property. Whatever the appraisal report states that the fair market value of the property is, is usually what they go by to determine what they're willing to pay for a particular property. They also take into account what the appreciation rate is in a specific area.

They ask the question: what is the property appreciating at five percent, ten percent, fifteen percent, etc. each year? What is the area of property appreciation? They want to know how it compares to the property appreciation rates in other areas. For example, if a property fair market value is $100,000.000 and property value in that area has been appreciating at 10 percent. That would mean that if you purchase the property, you're looking at for $100,000.000 it should increase in value by $10,000.00 (10%) making it at some point worth $110,000.00. They are content with being appreciation investors. But the problem with that is (as they experienced in 2008) for whatever reason, if the properties stop appreciating in value or if the housing market in the area being manipulated starts to plummet, then those investors are exposing themselves to a great deal of risk that could have been avoided based on the investment philosophy they relied on. And although the finance world and their associates would like to make it seem as though the community reinvestment act (see chapter 6) mandate created the foreclosure devastation; the truth of the matter is the housing market was manipulated by those who were legally obligated to maintain the integrity of the housing valuation and financing process.

This book is about keeping you from investing in such perilous (hazardous) manipulated housing markets. And by contrast, this is the characteristics of a Property Equity Niche Investor. The Property Equity Niche Investor does not invest outside of the urban communities. They do not rely solely on the fair market value of the property, because they invest in physically distressed properties in the inner-city. The Property Equity Niche Investor when valuing property to purchase first establishes what the As Is value of the property is , and then work from there discussed later in this chapter. They look to purchase the property below the As Is market value. Here's what the three separate and distinct dynamics are that make up The Property

Equity Niche Investor Approach. (1) The As Restored value of the property, (2) The As Is value of the property, and (3) The cash purchase price (p.p) which represents a steep discounted percentage of the As Is value of the property.

The restored value of the property is what it will be worth once the restoration work is completed. For example, let's say you found a two-family house with an appraised As Restored value of $115,000 dollars, and As Is value of $60,000 dollars and you purchased the property for cash at 40% below its As Is value for $24,000 dollars purchase price. That means you purchased a property with As Restored value of $115,000 for only $24,000.00. A 40% below its As Is value and percent below its as restored value. Only the property equity niche investing system will yield these kinds of returns on your invested dollars.

So that's 91,000 dollars of the property is equity plus the $24,000.00 invested for a total of $115,000.00 (the As Repaired value). Once you place your section 8 tenants in the property and establish a steady rental income source, you will then see the beauty in the apartment rental business. Obviously, this illustration does not cover every detail associated with the real estate investment process. But it was shown to help you understand the Property Equity Niche Investment System. (See chapter 27 on the six steps that make up this investment system).

Now let's explore another scenario in fuller detail. Even when the properties in the inner cities do start to depreciate (go down) in value, The Property Equity Niche Investment System safeguards you from any lost you would typically sustain as a conventional appreciation investor, because you brought the property at a percentage of its (As is value) not the As Restored value, or Fair market value. And even in the worst of inner-city housing markets, if the property you purchased depreciated in value by let's say 40% (not highly probable but possible) once it's up and operating, your capital investment in the property is well protected, because (very likely) that the existing equity in the property will not fall below the price you purchased the property for.

Unlike the conventional appreciation investor who invests hoping that the property appreciates (increases) in value. These types of real estate investors purchase property close to or right at its market value and then when the market dips in value guess what, so does the money used, placing the investor in the red (at a loss). For example, let's say you purchased property for $40,600. The As Restored value is $145,000, the As Is value is $75,000.00. Your purchase price represents 28% of the property as restored or fair market value. That means you purchased the property for 28% of its As Restored value. (40,600 divided into 198,000 multiplied by 100%= 28%). And now, let's say that the housing market in the area is hit by a housing meltdown (property values have aggressively declined) and the area properties are depreciating at 40% (again highly unlikely).

That means the same property worth $145,000 before has lost $58,000 in equity making it now worth $87,000. (145,000.00 x .40%= $58,000.00) 145,000 minus $58,000= $87,000. Remember your cash purchase price in the property is only $40,600. Now we look at how much of the property's equity spread is left. The property's current market value cash purchase of $87,000 in the property is $40,600 so we subtract $40,600 from $87,000 and we get $46,400. (that's in dollar figures) now let's look at it in percentage terms. Property equity spread remaining is $46,400 divided into 40,600 (your capital investment) multiplied by 100% equals 114% wow! Please tell me you caught it. If not it's okay by the time you're done not just reading but studying the investment principles in this book you will have caught it!

Now we are going to look at a simple illustration that exemplifies the rationale behind the Property Equity Niche Investment System. Note: The lower you, the property for, the higher the yield (rate of return) on the funds you used to purchase the real estate will be. Noticed I said funds that are committed to purchasing the real estate. This is not the same as your capital investment which includes additional cost factors (I.E. insurance, renovation cost, property inspections, appraised report title insurance search, etc. This illustration below shows the inverted (the reverse order) relationship between the funds you used to purchase the property and how the properties yield (rates of return) is affected by it.

The lower the property's purchase price.

The higher the equity return on your cash purchase price.

By contrast, the higher the cash purchase price.

The lower the equity return on your cash purchase price.

As a property equity niche investor, you will become knowledgeable of certain terminology, the principles that govern the Property Equity Niche Investing, and how it should be applied as it relates to this real estate investment system. Once again, the three essential components associated with this system have been listed below. The As Restored market value. Which represents the market value of the property once the renovation work is done. It also represents what your equity position will be in the property once the renovation work is completed. This is vitally important to this system, because at some juncture (point in time) you will be borrowing against the equity in the property to purchase additional properties. (See chapter 25) On Accessing the Equity in Your Property. The As is value (the value of the property in its current physical condition). The value of the property is what you determine it to be once your prequalification and valuation process has been completed, not what the seller, or even what market says it is. Remember that!

After going through the depreciated value accumulation technique, you then determine what the property's current "As Is" value is to you! The purchase price represents the amount of money you used to purchase the real estate. This is important because ideally the property's purchased price should be below its as is value! However, you would still be protected if you purchased it right at the As-is value mark.

Establishing a substantial equity position in a property purchased as an appreciation investor is virtually impossible to do. Because the increase in market value can only be hoped for after the property has been purchased. Versus as a Property Equity Niche Investor the property equity position is determined by you based on a qualifying and valuation system before you purchase the property. As a real estate Appreciation Investor, you are completely at the mercy of the variables that can manipulate the housing market. As a Property Equity Investor, you can not only better gauge and control the investment process, but you can position yourself to significantly gain from the purchase of the property.

Now do you see the major difference in each investment approach and how it can impact your bottom line (the return on your invested dollars). Remember this book is not intended to be the full scope of meeting your educational and investment learning needs. Its purpose is only meant to serve as the steppingstone which begins the process of elevating you to greater educational and financial heights!

Author's Thoughts: How many times have you said throughout life that you can do anything that you set your mind to? Well, the Property Equity Niche Investment Approach is for the one willing to apply themselves. The time has come to stop talking about it and start being about it. Learn it! Apply it! And then, Get paid for it!

3 Putting Together a Professional Team

Real Estate Attorney. When assembling a professional team make sure that the attorney specializes in the services you need him/her to do. Ask how long they have been practicing as a real estate attorney? Is he/she current on the landlord/tenant relationship laws in the state you reside in? Does he/she own investment property? This question is asked because you want to make sure that he/she is intimately acquainted with the real estate investment field as an investor and not just someone with a bunch of head knowledge. You don't want to choose an attorney who practices criminal law, with some knowledge of the real estate investment field. Also, you want to know how much you will be charged (i.e. by the hour, a flat rate per deal) etc.

The following is a list of services you want your real estate attorney to perform. This list is not exhaustive, it doesn't cover everything, but it covers the usual.

Services provided by the attorney:

- He/she will do a property title search. I would save the title insurance company for the inhabited properties.
- He/she should customize the tenant/landlord agreement in accordance with your objective and interests. As long as it doesn't violate any housing laws.
- He/she should become knowledgeable with the property equity niche investment approach.
- He/she should write-up the purchase sales agreement contract with the maximum protection on you that the laws allow.
- He/she has the responsibility of making sure that the title of the property legally passes to you.

- He/she should also be used for selling property (when you decide that's what you want to do.) Your realtor should also be a part of this process.
- He/she will make sure that the deed with your name on it is recorded in the City Hall property records department (known as the registrar of deed.)

If the city or private owner you're buying the property from, lawyer draws up the contract then it will be your attorney's responsibility to look it over and make sure that your interest is protected, and that it's not a unilateral contract. (Meaning it is a contract that favors the seller's interest entirely.)

Wherever the property acquisition closing is scheduled to take place make sure that your lawyer is going to accompany you. Many lawyers will try to convince their clients that they are capable of handling more than one function concerning real estate investment activities. (eg. Tax filing related issues and that may be so.) but if confronted with this type of situation kindly state, "I appreciate the offer but that particular interest of mine is being taken care of by someone else." You need their focus to be solely on real estate purchasing and selling issues. Nothing else! When looking for an accountant, ask how long they have been practicing as a real estate accountant. Are they current on the tax laws.? how do they charge, is it by the hour, per dialect. Do they have any investment property? Once you have determined that's definitely satisfied with his/her credentials, you're going to make him/her a part of your professional investment team. You should expect the following services:

- He or she should inform you on how to keep all your

documents concerning real estate expenses for tax filing time.

- make sure that you understand depreciation as it relates to investment property and how it serves as a tax shelter for the income that your property produces. Which in essence means that you will be able to keep a portion of it. If not all of the income that your property produces in the early years.
- He or she should explain this in detail to you.
- He or she should also advise you on tax deferral investments that the IRS allows. Tax deferral means that you put off to a later date paying the IRS the taxes you owe, so that you can put those dollars to work for you! Again, it's your accountant's responsibility to explain this to you.

Remember the information in this book is designed to give you the reader a basic framework of understanding concerning the real estate grind, who the parties are that are involved, and the housing entitlement programs created to provide you with financial assistance.

Realtor. Realtors are invaluable. they're a fountain of information in the real estate arena. Make sure you have one that is knowledgeable in mixed use properties as well as residential. This will be discussed in chapter 25. But I must inform you that for the most part (with few exceptions) they do not get excited about being a selling agent when it comes to distressed properties in the urban community. Why? Because their Commission is not much.

Remember they get paid on Commission. So, it would stand

to reason why they would prefer to be the selling agent in the middle to upper class areas because their Commission is much greater than what they would make on selling a property in the inner city. Even the banks that have foreclosed on properties in the inner cities will practically give them away to get them off of their books (through a process called short sale). Although there are few exceptions to the practice these Realtors already know (more often than not) who they're going to offload these properties to. The seasoned real estate investor considers its sound business practice to contact Realtors who may come across some distressed properties in the inner cities and inform them that they are interested in purchasing these kinds of properties.

I am going to share something else with you, these kinds of investors buy in bulk. So, if a realtor is selling 10 to 15 or more properties guess what, these investors are going to take every last one of the properties off of the Realtors hands for dirt cheap! Because remember as I stated to you in chapter one on Property Equity Niche Investing, there are a few exceptional investors that will invest in inner city properties. So, in this case, who do you think has a better chance at buying the property available, you or the investor who can afford to purchase them all?

Some investors use Realtors to get an approximate value of what inner city property values are for free. I recommend that you obtain the services of an appraiser when necessary.

Real Estate Appraiser. The market value of most if not all property is determined by the appraiser. For the inner-city distressed property, they are appraisers' services that can be obtained but it's not necessary all the time. Whatever you do, do not allow your appraiser to do a drive by appraisal. They have been known to do that in the urban community. Make sure they thoroughly evaluate the property before writing up an appraisal report. It would be wise of you to be present when this procedure is taking place. As a Property Equity Niche Investor there are two dynamics dealing with the property's value that you are concerned with.

1. The as Restored value

2. The As is value.

Make sure you request both. Each will be given a dollar amount, so you can estimate the properties goldmine potential once you have rehabilitated it. The As Restored market value is how much you can ask for the property if you were to place it on the market for sale once you have done the restoration. But in your case as a Section 8 housing provider, it just gives you an idea of what the property's value will be once you rehab it. This will just be your starting point when deciding how much you are willing to offer to purchase the property.

Contractor. Your tradesman. The one who will be responsible for fixing up your investment property. make sure this person is insured, bonded, and licensed so he /she can pull the permits to perform the job. And also ask if they are familiar with the apartment Section 8 ready process. When dealing with contractors you should always have a couple of them bid on the same project. And obviously the one that makes the lowest bid will be the one employed by you. Let whichever one contracted for the job know that you will be calling to make sure that he/she is legally operating as a tradesman as well as checking to see if their credentials are current (i.e, up to date).

Make sure you are given a project completion timeline with their estimate. Have them give you an itemized breakdown on how much their labor will cost you, and how much the material will cost. The reason you are asking for an itemized breakdown is because Some contractors (not all) have been known to inflate the material cost and make you issue them cash for that amount and then go and purchase the material and supplies from a supplier they have a tradesman discount with. They will pocket the dollar amount over what they actually paid for it and bring you back a receipt stating the retail value of the material cost. Meanwhile they use their tradesman discount to purchase the material. Not only do they pocket the excess funds, but they also claim it as a deduction on their income tax form during their tax. When that is your rightful expense. Your tax-deductible entitlement. This is why I recommend that you have the contractor you choose to itemize their labor cost as well as the material always incorporate into your renovation budget a 20% cost overrun allowance. Discuss with your real estate attorney about what's the proper payment plan to structure with your contractor. Have them draw up a standard contract for you to use when securing contract jobs.

Grant Writer. A grant writer is someone who can find you the money you need to meet the local affordable housing need. Grant riders are worth their weight in gold. Finding housing grant money for you is what they specialize in. Every municipality has its own version of a housing grant program. Unless Congress discontinued their funding which I doubt. My suggestion is to contact a housing grant writer in your area and make an appointment to speak with them face to face. Once you sit down with them, explain to them that you are interested in addressing the local affordable housing need by becoming a first-time landlord and that you will be renting to Section 8 approved individuals. Ask them directly what type of grant money is available.

Find out if they charge a contingency fee, which they should. Meaning that they only receive a fee if they are successful in securing the funds for you. In the event they do obtain the funds their fee should come out of those funds. Policies and criteria will vary from city to city, and state to state. It is always best to ask the right questions up front so you will know how to plan your pursuit. This path is worth exploring. Especially since the funds you receive are free. In chapter five you will learn about the source of the housing grant money.

Notary Public. A notary is an official authorized to certify or attest to (declare to be true) documents and takes affidavits. you will use this professional for all real estate related documents that by law need to be notarized. In Chapter 11 I will show you how they fit into your real estate investment system.

Property Insurance Agent. Once you become a property owner look into taking out investment property insurance. It consists of the following,

- **Hazard Insurance** -which protects you from risks such as fires or storms.
- **liability insurance**. Protects you from claims arising from injuries or damage to other people's property. Insurance on your investment property is not only the smart action to take, but also the only action to take that will place maximum protection on your investment. Consult a few insurance agents to see what type of

insurance coverage policy they suggest. When you're on a grind, every precautionary measure is taken to protect what you consider to be your assets. The real estate grind is no different!

Author's thoughts. I remember when I was a teenager our form of grind in the ville back then was playing craps, shooting pool for money, playing all types of card games, shiny shoes and whatever else presented an opportunity for us to make money. It was about stacking a dollar as we called it. If someone said to you, "let me hold something." It meant letting them borrow some money. The response would be I'm on a "Cincinnati grind" which was considered back then to be the most intensive grind one can be on. Translation "I don't have it to lend ".

That's what the real estate grind should mean to all of you already in the field or just starting out. Stack some money, reinvest some by purchasing more property, flip from time to time, buy and sell fast but always make sure you keep enough real estate in your portfolio to rent out. This way you will always have a strong cash flow coming in monthly. This method of grinding is like taking out additional insurance coverage against financial devastation!

4 Raising Private Capital Through Partnerships

Raising private capital in advance through a partnership is a smart thing to do. It would be prudent of you if you have some friend or family member to discuss with them the possibility of forming a partnership to invest in some distressed properties in the inner city. Recommend that they purchase this book so they can be enlightened to the gold mine that's accessible within the urban community. The alternative though, is if you have some money saved up in the bank, then try to find a couple of more people like you and pull your money together, create a partnership, and begin to qualify those professionals I talked about in chapter 3.

In this chapter you will be introduced to what is called a "Shared Equity Partnership Agreement." This is a partnership agreement that I have meditated on over the years for my personal real estate partnership deals. As a matter of fact, I have used this type of partnership for illustrative purposes in the classes I have taught. You don't necessarily have to use this one for the partnership you create. This one here is to just give you a type of partnership structure you could use when organizing a real estate Investment Partnership.

Once you understand the principles you will be able to effectively put together partnerships at any time and for different deals. Since you will be the one taking the lead on these deals you have to have a clear realistic vision. To see what the Shared Equity Partnership Agreement format looks like, see Appendix 1.

Try to keep your partners to no more than four people, including yourself when you first start out. Please make sure that all your agreements with others are placed in documentation form no matter how close you are to them! Sound business practices dictate that you place safeguard protection on yourself as well as others. You will be surprised how quickly people's recollection of their agreed upon investment becomes hazy once the money starts coming in. Note: consult your real estate attorney on what partnership structure will best fit your real estate investment objectives. See chapter 18 on real estate investment clubs. In the next chapter I will provide you with an example on how to determine the return of your investment dollar.

Author notes: being cash strapped (in need of money) should not be a hindrance for you to invest in real estate. Once you have obtained the knowledge, wisdom and understanding that this book contains, you will be able to not only invest in but through capital raising, obtain the money you will need to purchase property in the inner cities. Don't let that "I don't currently have the money mentality" keep you in economic despair. Learn this six-step systematic approach to being a Property Equity Niche Investor. Learn how to raise the capital you will need to invest in real estate and then make it work for you. It's just that simple.

5 The HUD Financial Assistance Program

In this chapter I have included the housing programs that I am aware of. As I stated in the forward, this book and its information is not exhaustive. So, after reading this book make sure you diligently research what all your municipalities have to offer by way of real estate and housing assistance. Remember each state or city will have its own name for some programs, although the same principle will be applied. That is to make available funds for affordable housing.

For starters, let's look at what the Housing and Urban development department function is. Created in September of 1965 it is a U S government agency established to implement certain Federal Housing and community development programs. This federal agency attempts to assure decent, safe, and sanitary housing for all Americans. It investigates complaints of discrimination and housing. Example: Tim wants to develop a housing project for low-income families. He applies to the Department of Housing and Urban Development for a special low interest loan for the development.

A lot of the housing development that takes place in the urban communities are funded by the Housing and Urban development department. The local developers love this government financed program. Now let's look at a program titled Community Development Block Grant or CDBG.

Title 1 of the Housing and Community Development Act of 1974 gives the authority to provide annual grants known as Community Development Block Grants to entitle cities and counties. The purpose of these grants are to develop communities by providing decent housing, suitable living environments and expanding economic opportunities, principally for low and moderate income persons. Grants are awarded to entitlement communities or (urban communities) to carry out a wide range of community development activities directed toward Neighborhood Revitalization, economic development and the provision of improved community facilities and services.

Activities must meet one of the following three national objectives:

1. To benefit low- and moderate-income persons Earning less than 80% of the area median income.
2. To aid in the prevention or the elimination of slums and blight, ruined property, in the inner cities.
3. To meet an urgent need, imminent threat, and natural disaster.

This information above comes directly from the Housing and Urban development Agency. At this writing the 2012 national budget plan consisted of cutting some of the funding allocated to this program. Which means that if passed it is once again the urban communities that are made to be the Sacrificial Lamb. Check with your respective economic development agency to see how much of an increase or decrease in funding the program did they receive. Always follow the money. Here are a few more eligible activities under the CDBG program:

Acquisition of real property. Property to be acquired must be viewed in terms of the planned use of the property involved for purposes of evaluating compliance with the CDBG national objectives.

Relocation. Used for relocation payments or assistance to displace persons, families or businesses.

Housing Rehabilitation. To finance the rehabilitation of any public or privately owned residential property, including the conversion of nonresidential property for housing.

Special Economic Development Activities. Commercial or industrial improvements or assistance to private and for-profit entities in the form of loans. This program is for the more established businessman or businesswoman; however, if you are already educated on such matters and ambitious enough, look into the criteria to qualify.

In the area I'm from a lot of the Community Development Block Grant disbursements are made available as a result of revitalization zone committees. These organized committees are responsible for some of the housing development that takes place in their designated revitalize zone areas. Most savvy real estate investors seek the support of Neighborhood Revitalization Zone committees to help them secure the Community Development Block Grant money when renovating or developing housing in the inner city.

This program is ideal for your housing grant writer covered in Chapter 3. They can be very instrumental in obtaining these funds. Remember this is what they specialize in. Check into HUD' Reunification Program. The U. S. Department of Housing and Urban Development recently announced a $20 million in funding to local housing authorities to help more than 2500 families stay together, it's estimated that the awarded rental vouchers will reunite nearly 5000 children with their parents or prevent them from entering foster care in the first place HUD reports.

This text is quoted from Hertz Secretary Shaun Donovan, "the foster care system is an important safety net for children when there's no alternative but not having the means to obtain affordable housing it's hardly a good reason for families to be divided." I concur! "Thankfully these vouchers will keep thousands of families together under one roof." HUD's Family unification program will make 2,543 housing choice vouchers available for families whose inadequate housing is the primary cause of their separation from their children.

In addition, 20% of these vouchers will provide stable housing for approximately 750 young adults from ages 18 to 22, who are aging out of the foster care system, preventing them from becoming homeless. I added this information for two reasons. 1.) For you to check and see if this program has been instituted in your area. 2.) For you to see how dreadful the affordable housing availability in America is, and how it can directly affect the family. This should bring more meaning to the gold mines in your neighborhood waiting to be mined by you! This info should be compelling enough for you to contact HUD's Section 8 department and ask the staff member in charge of the Section 8 program waiting list, how many approved applicants are waiting for an available apartment to rent out. The numbers will blow your mind!

This is why the Real Estate Grind is truly The Inner City's Gold Mine! Now let's look at where else the HUD funds are. HUD's 203K program is sponsored by the Federal Housing Administration department. The Federal Housing Administration, created in 1934 is an agency within the United States Housing and Urban Development that administers many loan programs, loan guarantee programs and loans insurance programs, designed to make more housing opportunities available. In essence HUD's 203K program provides you with the purchasing and rehabilitation money. The Federal Housing Administration, FHA, insures the loan amount you the borrower receives from the lender. Please do not take me including this HUD program information in this chapter as an endorsement. I do not recommend that you start off investing in real estate by using this above-mentioned program. I only included this information to give you knowledge on another government sponsored program that I am aware of, and that's available to real estate investors. However, the Community Development Block Grant Program is money you can obtain without having to pay it back. If you qualify. I am sure that there are other government sponsored programs available as well for real estate investors. So be sure to check into it, at least for your personal knowledge's sake.

Author's Thoughts: lack of knowledge is extremely hazardous to one's mental, social and economic being. Not knowing immobilizes, paralyzes and serves as the barrier to the individual's chance to prosper. Because in order for any investor to be effective in a particular field, they have to first possess the capability and aptitude (know how) concerning their investment field of interest. The more knowledge they have in that respective field, the more effective they can be. In this book I have provided you with an investment system, as well as additional information to start you off as a beginner in the real estate investment field. I have also encouraged you to increase your knowledge, as it pertains to real estate investing by purchasing other books that deal with this same topic, and to also search the local Housing and Urban Development online site to find out if there have been any new real estate investors programs implemented. Remember as I stated to you previously knowledge is power Only when aptly applied!

Information on government sponsored programs was taken from www.hud.gov

6 The Community Reinvestment Act

This chapter is about revealing to you one of the best kept secrets in the urban community for the last 34 years as of this writing. By the end of this chapter there will be those of you that will be saying, "How come I haven't heard about this community Reinvestment Act before the writing of this book"? After you get over the shock of it, take what you learned here, further your education on it, and then utilize it to your benefit!

Now let's get down to business. What is the Community Reinvestment Act all about? Community reinvestment act, CRA, is an act passed by Congress in 1977 to encourage the financial institutions to meet the credit needs of the community in which they operate, the urban community. To ensure the banks in the inner cities comply with the federal mandate compliance is monitored by way of regular audits by federal regulators, and a poor record of CRA compliance is taken into consideration when the financial institution applies for deposit facilities (other banks), including merger and acquisitions.

Before we proceed, I want to elaborate a little more on the Community Reinvestment Act for your clear understanding about its creation and function. As the definition states it is an act passed by Congress in 1977 that mandated that every federally Chartered Bank that is established in the urban community reinvest a percentage of its funds back into the community it serves. What should be troubling to anyone that is now reading this part of the book is that Congress had to take firm action in making sure that these banks that were set up in the urban neighborhoods made loans available to those residents in the community that they served.

This action by Congress represents a reaction to what was the overt (obvious) problem. This systematic discriminatory lending practice perpetrated by these banks against the inner-city community residents was called Redlining. Redlining is an illegal practice of a lender refusing to make loans in certain areas, the inner city. The term comes from circling with a red pencil on a map in the areas where the institution will not lend. When this occurs mortgage financing is denied, property values spiral downwards, which ultimately creates urban blight. Now don't get me wrong, I am not accusing any Bank of presently operating this way. But what I am endeavoring to do in this chapter, is explain to you what gave birth to the Community Reinvestment Act being passed. Under this act Redlining is now outlawed!

Another definition states the refusal of home mortgages to areas or neighborhoods judged to be poor financial risk. So, to put this information in its proper context these are the facts that up until 1977 the banks were systematically denying those inner-city residents judged to be poor financial risk. Obviously, somebody or bodies took issue with this maltreatment based on socioeconomic and geographic discriminatory practices and brought it to the attention of Congress who responded with a law to ensure that those discriminated against would finally receive equitable lending treatment. This information on the Community Reinvestment Act, and on the bias redlining practice is well documented for you to explore for yourself, and I suggest that you do just that!

Then ask yourself how much has really changed. In light of this legislation banks now have a legal responsibility to make loans available to you. If you don't assert your right, it will continue to go unnoticed. As of this writing pressure is being placed on the banks by the federal government to make sure that the banks are complying with the Community Reinvestment Act mandate. Which brings me to my next point: those of you who are not registered voters, need to become registered. Why? Because it's the job of your elected officials, house of representatives and senators from your state to represent your interest when they're on Capitol Hill.

They are supposed to make sure that your express will is carried out. But if you're not registered to vote or are registered and do not vote, then it's like you're saying to the politicians that represent you, do what you feel is best for me. Instead of you communicating by the candidate you endorse what's best for you. You must become more politically involved! Find out about the candidate that is asking you to vote for them. Do their views line up with your personal views? What is their track record? Remember, based on the constitution this is supposed to be a government of the people, for the people, and by the people. So, make sure that your voice is heard through the elected official you send to Washington DC.

That's a little of the political content I foretold you of in the introduction. Now the question becomes how can these CRA funds be assessed to aid someone interested in real estate property investment? Most, if not all municipalities have what is known as Urban Renewal Zoned areas. Check out this urban renewal definition: rehabilitation of slum neighborhoods in the urban areas as replacement or rehabilitation of substandard buildings. Although not stated, the Urban Renewal initiative is a good choice for acquiring Community Reinvestment Act bank financing. Since this entire book is about the Real Estate Grind being the Inner City's Gold Mine, I'm going to Illustrate to you how the funding can be obtained.

Example: only after gaining a sound understanding of the real estate investment system this book promotes do I recommend that you target the urban renewal zoned areas in the inner city. Check out the Small Business Administration to see if they offer free assistance. Also check in your state and city to see if there are any nonprofit organizations that offer free assistance in preparing a business plan. The Internet can be very helpful in this matter as well. Once a business plan writer is found, inform them up front that you will be requesting CRA financial assistance and that the CRA requested funds are going to be used for addressing the urban renewal zone housing initiative. It should be explained that the money will be used for buying properties, rehabilitating it and then renting it out to Section 8 approved applicants. Once the business plan is written, make an appointment to speak with the bank branch manager.

Step two. Schedule an appointment with the branch manager in advance, that's how business is handled, expect to cover the nature of the appointment with them. The fact that CRA funds are being sought after means that the person seeking it must be polished enough to clearly articulate their position. Once the meeting comes around, it should be expressed that the interest rate must be fixed, no adjustable rate.

Step three. Once the loan has been approved the property found, filing with the Housing Authority Section 8 department would be wise. Word of caution: I share these steps with you only for mental visualization. In no way should you get the impression I am recommending that you pursue this route as a beginner real estate investor. When seeking financing through a bank you're dealing with a different type of animal. At this moment, I am not speaking to you as the author of this book. I have now changed hats and put on my overprotective Big Brother hat!

So, before you take a plunge into this water, make sure you or someone you know is capable of swimming in the deep end period. Now that you have some understanding of what the Community Reinvestment Act is all about. It's your responsibility to study more on it, sharpen up your real estate investment skills, and then put together a real estate investment plan that will allow you to secure those CRA available funds. In the beginning of this chapter, I asked the question, "What should the Community Reinvestment Act mean to you?" If I have done my job this information should have sparked a change of interest on your part to know more about it.

Author's thoughts: as I mulled over the urban community state of affairs, as it is today, I am more convinced that a lot of my brothers and sisters are in desperate need of an epiphany, (a sudden understanding or revelation), concerning their multi facet condition. They have been looking at life through a lens that breeds complacency, dependency, and resistance to substantive change! Someone once said to me, "If you always do what you've always done, you can always expect the same outcome." It's time to make a change!

7 Your Landlord/Tenant State Laws

This is a subject where you definitely cannot afford to be uninformed. Therefore, touch bases with your real estate attorney and have him or her walk you through the landlord tenant relationship legal requirement before you enter into a lease agreement with any prospective tenant. As you will see, I have listed below the most common state laws as it relates to the landlord tenant relationship.

- Discrimination-you cannot discriminate against an individual solely on the basis of the persons race, religion or sex. This type of practice violates the fair Housing Act provisions.
- Holding deposits. Some states require landlords to keep security deposits in a separate bank account and the entire interest that the account accumulates is the tenants, while in other states the landlord is entitled to a percentage of the interest that's attributed to the separate accounts. Inquire to your attorney about what your state law says about these issues. Know that some states will not allow a landlord to charge nonrefundable security deposits. Also, you have to consider what type of security deposits you are going to ask for, versus what the Housing Authority Section 8 program will allow.
- Disclosures. Disclosures will have to Be made about lead and other substances in the building. **Caution:** If the property you purchased was built in the 70s or before there is a high probability that it's lead contaminated, because during those times lead based paint was used on houses.

As a landlord you will also qualify tenants through a process called Tenant Selection. This includes what criteria you are going to set for determining who you will accept and who you will reject.

Author thoughts: the title of this chapter couldn't be more fitting. Your dealing with your tenant is truly a relationship. And just like any other relationship that's built on trust and respect, this one is no different. Always remember that each party has a responsibility to the other. You, the landlord, have a responsibility to provide the tenant with a safe and operable living environment. By comparison, the tenant is responsible for making sure your property is taken care of, and that you receive their percentage of the rent on time they're required to pay period. I recommend that you always respond swiftly in addressing tenants' complaints, in order to avoid unnecessary inconveniences!

8 Valuing the Property: What It's Worth to You

Since primarily the properties that you will be targeting will not be producing income initially, the valuation method covered in this chapter is to help you understand how typically property is valued. When you are in a commercial business grind mode you take into account the perceived value of a product, its cost and then based on that product's demand and resale potential you arrive at a predetermined profit margin found on a mathematical procedure. The real estate grind is no different!

In the real estate investment field, you must be able to determine approximately beforehand the return potential on your invested dollar. The three valuation methods listed below have been integrated into the Property Equity Niche Investment Approach, for satisfying maximum results. A lot of times when people invest in real estate, they will pay entirely too much for it, and as a result they don't experience the maximum return on their investment dollar. So I have put together a valuation system that takes into account the different sources out there to protect all would-be investors from making the same mistake that many that came before them made. This book is about simplifying and guiding you down a safer fruitful path. Once you have developed your real estate investment skills, you can step up the grind by purchasing properties more aggressively!

Now let's look at the three valuation approaches.

Sales Comparable Analysis. This valuation approach can involve all or one of the home valuation websites. (i.e., Trulia.com, Zillow.com etc.)

For example, let's say you found an abandoned two-family

dwelling that has two bedrooms in each unit, one bathroom, one kitchen and one living room. You will know this information because you looked at the property records located in the county's land record office. Note: this is also some of the same information that will be entered on the property prequalification worksheet.

This valuation approach is good for two reasons the information you obtain is free. It gives you an idea of what the property's restored value can potentially be once renovations are done on it. Know that this valuation method cannot be applied in every case because for whatever reason the house valuation website may not have the info. That's when another valuation approach will have to be applied.

The next valuation approach is to utilize the services of an appraiser. What is an appraiser? An appraiser is one who is qualified through their education and experience to estimate the value of real estate. They issue what is called an appraisal report. What is an appraisal report? An appraisal report is a written explanation of a property value, including the data and reasoning used to determine that value. Appraisal reports are used to determine a reasonable offer price because they can give you the as is Value and the As Restored value. These two valuation components listed above are very important to you as a Property Equity Niche Investor. It also breaks down what the land value and the building value is separately. In some cases, the fee paid to an appraiser is money well spent by you. The Property Equity Niche Investment Approach has been designed to work in an integrated way with all the valuation methods, to provide you with a buffer that will ensure a competitive return on your investment.

The last conventional valuation approach is called The Replacement Cost Approach or Cost Approach. What is the Replacement Cost Approach? It's the cost of erecting a building to replace or serve the function of a previous structure. Your investment property insurance policy should have a replacement cost section in it. The insurance company includes this section in your insurance policy to inform you of what monetary compensation to expect from them, in the event your existing property suffers total loss.

When real estate is in a deteriorated condition and located in a declining urban area it affects the entire real estate. Both the building and land value in this author's opinion, there is a direct relationship between the real estate and the declining area where it is located. Therefore, as a property equity nice investor your valuation method must account for this fact. Here's my reasoning behind this answer. Before land is developed it's assigned a value based on its square footage and its highest and Best Use.

There are other factors taken into account, such as the area the land is located in. What type of building will be developed? What does the land development in that particular area cost as it relates to a specific type of development? How much of the housing market demand is there for this type of development? What price will the end product in this case a residential unit be able to command in price? Is this particular type of development in this area on the rise, decline, or nonexistent?

These are some important questions that each and every real estate investor should answer before making an investment decision! Land value is based on square footage, highest and best use which should bring about the highest price, its desirability once the end product is complete, how much investment interest will it generate, and its marketability, will selling it quickly and at the predetermined price be too much of a challenge. So now the question becomes what if physically the building part of the real estate has deteriorated significantly leaving it in a state of despair, all the surrounding properties are rundown, and the area is saturated with vacant lots. As a result of all this there is no investment interest in the area.

All these factors will surely affect the land value. Sensible reasoning would suggest that if the highest and best use, desirability and marketability was used to originally determine the land value, then deterioration of these listed elements would most certainly negatively affect its value significantly! Now before I proceed, I would like to take the time out to introduce you to a term called Depreciated Value Accumulation. What is the depreciated accumulation value? It is the least amount of real estate value in the building.

The real estate the building value is allocated a percentage. For example, 75% and the land value is allocated a percentage for example 25%. These two percentages combined equal 100% of the real estate total value. Now for the sake of you understanding this process, take a look at the following scenario. Let's say you came across an abandoned two unit building that the pre-qualification process revealed was constructed 25 years ago. Just so you know the IRS Internal Revenue Service has a term called Depreciation.

What is depreciation? It is the loss of the building's value only based upon wear and tear over 27.5 years. If it is a two to four family residential property, starting from the day the real estate is purchased extending over a 27.5 year. If the property changes ownership the 27.5-year depreciation term resets according to the IRS. Also, according to the IRS the depreciation principle of 27.5 years is not applied to the land because it is their position that land does not depreciate in value overtime. But emphasis added, as a Property Equity Niche Investor you are not governed by or influenced by this depreciation principle. The IRS applies when you're prequalifying and valuing real estate to purchase. However, you must honor this government stipulation when it's tax filing time with your tax expert. Depending on the situation, you will use this depreciated accumulation value method. While in other situations you will rely on the Sales Comparison Analysis, or appraisal report. Rarely will the replacement cost method be used.

The depreciated accumulation value method takes the combined accumulated last value of the building and the land and subtracts it from the market value given of the real estate when it was first developed the remaining value is the as is value. Right now, let's take a look at this scenario using the accumulated depreciation value methods.

Let's say you come across an abandoned 2-unit property that the pre-qualification process revealed was developed 25 years prior. That means based upon the IRS building depreciation principle it has 2 1/2 years of value left from when it was first constructed. The property was appraised at $110,000 when the building was first constructed in 1987. 25 years as of 2012 which means that based upon the depreciation principle of 27.5 years, the property now has 2 1/2 years left of value in it. The building's value allocated percentage is 75% and the land value allocated percentage is 25%. Its preexisting city tax debt is $15,000, this figure includes interest and penalties (which is a lot of times negotiable). Request that the penalties and interest be forgiven by the tax collector. If you are successful, then secure a contract with the property's owner to buy their ownership interest in the property. So based upon this recorded information and factoring in the respective allocated percentage, the building and land value would look like this:

Building value- $82,500 (75% of $110,000)

Land value- $27,500 (25% of $110,000)

For a total $110000.00

Now using the depreciated accumulation value method, you have to determine what the present As is value of both the building and the land. The original building value of 82,500 divided by 27.5 years equals $3000 x 2.5 years = $7500. This figure represents the property as is value.

The original land value of $27,500 divided by 27.5 years equals $1000 x 2.5 years = $2500. This figure represents the land As Is value.

The building as is value of $7500 + the land As is value of $2500 = $10,000. This figure represents the real estate total as is valued.

Now remember the IRS says that land does not depreciate in value but from a Property Equity Niche Investor standpoint, because you are using your own valuation method to determine what the property is worth to you. You must operate in a way that protects you from paying too much for real estate in despair and located in deteriorated areas. Now in this case in order for you to determine what your purchase offer is going to be it's imperative that you contact the property owners of record to express your interest in buying this particular property. You should also request their permission to access the inside of the property, so that you can perform your due diligence order, a property title search, property inspection, and an appraisal report. You also want to give your contractor an opportunity to look at the property also.

Once you have carried out your due diligence , and are satisfied with the results , and you know the properties As is value, its restored market value and how much the restoration cost is going to be, you are now prepared to put together an offer to purchase contract to present to the property owner/s. Remember, as long as there is no structural damage to the property or any type of contamination it's a go. Close out the deal!

Here's what the total layout looks like for this investment project.

<u>Due Diligence</u>

Title Search - $250

Property Inspection - $4500

Appraisal Report - $350

Renovation Project Cost - $10,000

Plus - $11,050

20% renovation budget and allowance of $2000 making your renovation budget $12,000.

Investors Note: always incorporate a 20% cost allowance into your renovation budget in case during the renovation phase other damages are discovered. The Tax Collector agreed to forgive the interest and penalties, which brought the pre-existing tax debt to $7000.

The building allocated percentage value is 75% (110,000.00 x .75% = $82,500. The Land allocated percentage value is 25% (110,000.00 x .25% = $27,500.00) for a combination of $110,000.00. You can decide that $15,000 is a reasonable purchase offer. So based on the information gathered from both the prequalification and valuation process you presented, an offer to purchase contract was put together by you and presented to the property owner for $15,000. Your offer is accepted! Now take the to bring the signed contract to your lawyer, so that the title can be prepared in your name and recorded at the town county City Hall registry of deeds department.

Then go and take out investment property insurance on your newly acquired real estate. Since the owners abandoned the property and were willing to walk away from it and let the city foreclose on it due to tax delinquency and receive nothing if that should happen. You offering to purchase the property for $15,000 is a very generous offer. Obviously now you have to go to the Tax Collector's office with a copy of the deed and settle the agreed upon $7000 tax debt. But what happens if you are unsuccessful in contacting the property owners of record? See Chapter 23.

Investors Notes: remember what makes you a property Equity Niche Investor is the fact that you target to purchase deteriorated properties located in the inner cities, for way below its As Restored market value.

Recouping The Numbers

Your real estate purchase price $15,000

The tax principal debt settlement of $7000, renovation of $10,000, property title search $250 property inspections $450, and attorney fees $1200, are all costs associated with the property purchase.

Now let's look at what the real estate equity return is on your cash purchase.

$90,000 (Is restored market value based on the sales comparable analysis)
-$15,000 (Cash Purchase) =
$75,000 (This Figure represents the real estate equity return on your cash purchase expressed as a dollar amount.

Below is what the real estate equity return is on your cash purchase, expressed as a percentage using the Ratio and Proportion mathematical operation.

Part $75,000 divided by
Whole $15,000 100% equals a 500 % return on your cash purchase.

Wow!!!

This is why it makes investment sense to learn how to become a Property Equity Niche Investor.

Having stated that, what if the property's building value has been completely depleted, used up, based upon the IRS depreciation factor of 27.5 years. Looking at it from a Property Equity Niche Investment perspective, how does it affect the land value? And what valuation approach should you use? For instance, let's say the 27.5 years building depreciation allowance has been used up, and the rundown building is now in its 30th year since it was constructed. What feasible approach should you take?

In such a situation the valuation approach for you would be to obtain a sales comparable analysis. any time the property pre-qualification process reveals that an abandoned property's 27.5 years depreciation allowance has expired, request sales compare analysis to determine the properties as restored market value. Whatever the sales comparison analysis states the As Repaired value is you will purchase the property at 35% of that figure or you can obtain an appraisal in such cases.

Caution. I strongly recommend that you do not attempt to enter any property without permission from the property owners, because it will be considered trespassing, which is against the law! What are some of the legal ways you can explore to locate the property owners of record when investing in inner city abandoned real estate?

1. You can go through the neighborhood and attempt to find out if anyone is still in contact with the property owners. If they are, ask them would they mind giving you the owners name., Inform the person you're speaking with that you are interested in purchasing that particular property, and if it would be possible for them to relay this message. Give the person your name and contact number.
2. You can see if the property owner's phone number is listed in the telephone book or see if the information 411 operator has a listed number.
3. You can take out an ad in the local newspaper expressing your desire to get in touch with these owners to discuss the possibility of you buying that particular property that

is located at said property address.

4. You can attempt to locate the property owners by Googling the names on the property records.
5. You can see if the owners of record give the post office a forwarding mailing address.

If these above-mentioned attempts fail, try to work something out with the city's tax collector to purchase the property once they foreclose on it. Depending on what state you reside in, the local government may or may not be open to your purchase pitch. But nevertheless, try anyway! Below I have included the golden rule when dealing with the city on tax debt.

Author's Thoughts: Valuation as it relates to investing in real estate has been misrepresented by some who claim to be experts on the subject. As a result, many trusting, unsuspected, wannabe investors have had to face financial ruin. But what you need to be aware of is that in order for someone to have a realistic chance of being successful investing in real estate, there has to be a valuation approach, amongst other factors, that can serve as a microscopic lens in identifying the hidden value potential. Having stated that, I'm confident that the Property Equity Niche Investment Approach will provide you with the understanding and ability to operate in a safe and productive way. Shielding you from the location, location, location mindset that conventional real estate investors would have you buy into!

Golden Rule

When addressing the issue of pre-existing tax debt, the following two steps should always be explored.

1. See if the state you live in has a Tax Amnesty Program.

This means that if you purchase the property, you will not be responsible for paying off the pre-existing tax debt. In such a case, you may be able to purchase the property for one dollar.

2. If not, Request that the preexisting tax debt buildup of penalties and compound interest are forgiven or canceled in lieu of you agreeing to pay up the remaining principal balance. Be prepared to put a percentage down on it and make payments on it over a specified amount of time until the entire debt is paid.

Note: If the respective municipality does not agree to either of the above listed terms then you will have to determine if it still makes sense to go through with it.

Valuation Approach Worksheet #1

In this valuation approach, called the Depreciated Value Accumulation Approach, the real estate original appraised values, and the number of years that have passed since the building or land improvement was completed play a key role. In essence, the formal below is how you would value a city owned, abandoned properties.

1. State the value of the real estate once the building construction was completed.
2. Determine what the value allocation percentage is for the land and the building separately.
3. Apply the IRS depreciation method of 27.5% to the building value. Land is not depreciated, so whatever the land value was when the building was constructed on it remains the same. This you do by dividing the building value by 27.5 years. The figure you get represents an

annual figure spread out over 27.5 years.

4. Next you take the annual figure and multiply it by how many years have passed since the construction of the building.
5. The figure you get represents the amount of value that the real estate building has lost over the specified number of years.
6. The remaining amount of value for the building is then added to the initial land value and the sum total represents the as is value of the real estate.
7. Then you would consider what the pre-existing tax is. If it is less than the property as is value this may present a good investment opportunity for you. However, if the pre-existing tax debt is more than the properties as is value then apply the golden rule discussed earlier in chapter 8.

Valuation Approach Worksheet #2

Sales Comparison Analysis

This valuation approach is for properties with completely depleted depreciated value accumulation.

1. Obtain a sales comparable analysis.
2. This figure becomes the As Repaired property value.
3. Discount this figure 65% the remaining 35% represents the as is value of the property.
4. If you are purchasing directly from the city, compare this above figure to the properties total preexisting tax debt.
5. Is it more or less?
6. Were you successful in negotiating a successful tax reduction?
7. If yes, list it.

8. if it is less than you are ahead of the investment curve and this figure qualifies as your suggested cash purchase offer.

<u>Alternative scenario</u>

- If both of the property owners and the city are involved, use the As is property value figure is the ceiling for your cash purchase offer and or tax that settlement combined should not exceed the figure. (i.e. the as is property value)
- Property cash purchase
- Pre-Existing tax debt settlement if applicable total capital investment.

Value Approach Worksheet #4

Appraisal Report

1. Request and appraisal report
2. List the property appraised "as repaired" value.
3. List the properties appraised "as is" value.
4. Then subtract 25% off of that. This number becomes your suggested cash purchase offer.
5. Include the tax debt settlement in this equation also.

Note. In some cases, this figure will represent the property's cash purchase price.

9 Purchasing Inner City Distressed Properties

What does it consist of?

This step begins after you have gone through the prequalifying and valuation steps. Now pay careful attention to what I am about to share with you in this chapter, because it is key to the Property Equity Niche investment concept. In order for you to tie up the property, meaning to establish a position of control so that no one can come behind you and buy the property you're interested in, it's imperative that you locate the property owners of record. (See Chapter 8) At this point they still have ownership interest in the property or contact the tax collector if the city has already foreclosed on the property.

You start off by searching the property's record. All you have to do is enter the property address on the prequalification worksheet. If you are successful in finding the property owner's record, your chances of buying the property increases.

OK let's say there's a tax debt and utility debt on the property. Write down how much is owed.

Example:

Tax debt $________________

Utility debt $________________

Other debt $________________

$________________, $________________, $______________.

Note. The illustration above is an abbreviated layout just to make the point. As a matter of practice, call the representative for the utility companies to see if you will incur the pre-existing utility on the property if you should purchase it. Now the journey begins to find the property owners on record. (See Chapter 8)

When, and if contact is made with the property owners, request permission to access the inside of the property so you can begin the due diligence process. What is due diligence? It is an evaluation that often precedes the actual purchase of the property. This process considers the properties current physical condition, its market value potential, what type of liens are on the property, and the cost to renovate it. If the property owners agree to sell the property, take out your offer to purchase a sales agreement. Always keep this document with you for situations like this and give a down payment on the property. Use a check that states deposit down payment on property, not to be cashed until due diligence has been satisfied. Don't worry about the contract language, your real estate attorney will take care of this.

Your due diligence in this case will be to carry out a property title search through your attorney, or a title search company. Once this has taken place, you will then order the appraisal report, and then an inspection report. In this case I used an appraisal report, because I wanted to show you how various conventional valuation methods can be used together with the Property Equity Niche Investment approach. Also, at this point you will have your contractor assess what restoration work needs to be done. Once the appraisal report sets the As is and As Restored value, you will then discount the As is Valued by 25%, and then factor in your tax debt settlement with the city. The 25% represents your cash purchase offer to the property owners.

The reason why you use this valuation purchase offer format is so that you can pay the least amount to buy the property but receive the maximum market equity return on your money. Once the property owners sign the offer to purchase a contract, you will then control the property. Not own it but control it! Putting you in the driver seat. The offer to purchase contract should read along the lines of:

I ____________will give the property owners, ____________ 10% down payment of the purchase price and the remaining balance once, and if all due diligence conditions are found to be satisfying by the prospective buyer(you). If all conditions are not met the down payment must be returned to the prospective buyer upon his request.

Write in the contract that you will need 14 business days to perform your due diligence. Also included in the contract will be the closing date. Once the property owners signed the contract, write a check for the down payment and note in the check memo section down payment on property purchase. Notice that the language in the contract states that if all due diligence is found to be satisfying to the prospective buyer the remaining balance will be given. What this language basically means is if any of the reports, the inspection Report or appraisal report, are not satisfying you can nullify the offer to purchase contract and your down payment must be returned to you without delay when requested.

All you have to do is stay on the contract, "The condition section prospective buyer does not find that the contract conditional requirements to purchase the property to be satisfying." But like I will consistently encourage you to do throughout this book consult your real estate attorney so that the safeguard protection you need is part of the contract language. By contrast if you find that the reports are to your satisfaction give the property owners their remaining balance, pay up any negotiable pre-existing debt amount you agreed to pay for the property, and take full ownership of the property.

Congratulations! You are now a property owner.

Property Equity Niche Investment Economics 101

Now since this chapter is about buying inner city distressed properties let's recap the investment principal you learned in Chapter 2: On Property Equity Niche Investing. The higher the cash purchase of the real estate to its “As Restored value”; the lower the real estate equity return on your cash purchase. By contrast, the lower the cash purchase of the real estate to its “As Restored value”; the higher the real estate equity return on your cash purchase.

What is the real estate equity return? It's the difference between what the real estate As Restored value is minus your cash purchase. It is expressed in dollars, as well as percentages. It is a built-in real estate equity return until you borrow against it.

Investors Note. Commit this investment principle to memory. An illustration of this investment principle is as follows:

Illustration #1

You found a two-family property and determined that through an appraisal report it has an As Repaired value of $150,000, and an As is value of $70,000 and you purchased the property for $17,500 cash. Once you've completed the restorations on the property you will have received an equity return of $132,500 on the properties purchase price of $17,500. The equity returns on your $17,500 cash purchase expressed as a percentage return would be 757.14%.

Always subtract your cash purchase from the real estate As Restored value first, then take the remaining value and set the two figures up in a ratio and proportion format as shown below. (More Coverage on ratio and proportion in Chapter 12) Your cash purchase of $17,500 subtracted from the real estate As Restored value of $150,000 equals $132,500. This figure represents the real estate equity return on your cash purchase.

<u>$132,500 = 757.14%</u>
$17,500 = 100%

See chapter 12 on determining the return on your invested dollars to fully understand the ratio and proportion process.

Illustration #2

By contrast let's say you found a two-family property that has a restored value of $150,000 based on the appraised report you had done. And an as is value of $70,000 and you purchased the property for $60,000 cash, 40% of the as restored value. Once you've completed the restoration on the property you will have received a real estate equity return of $90,000 on your cash purchase of $60,000. The real estate equity returns on your $60,000 cash purchase expressed as a percentage would be 150%.

<u>$90,000 = 150%</u>

$60,000 = 100%

How do you determine the real estate equity percentage return? You divide the real estate equity return by the cash purchase, and times it by 100. For instance, 90,000 divided by 60,000 x 100 = 150%.

In the first scenario you receive a 757.14% real estate equity return on your cash purchase because you purchased the property at 11.67% of its As Restored value. 150,000 / 60,000 x 100 = 40%.

This is why it is so essential for you to fully understand the inverted effect, (the opposite direction), of purchasing property at a high price, which translates into a lower real estate equity return on your cash purchase. Versus buying it at a lower price which translates into a higher real estate equity return on your cash purchase.

Note. This above stated real estate equity return principle is based solely upon the Property Equity Niche Investment Approach when purchasing real estate. It does not take into account restoration or due diligence costs.

When a property owner fails to pay their property taxes, the tax collector at some point will place a tax lien on the property. A tax lien is debt attached to the property because the owner fails to pay their taxes. A tax lien can be imposed for failure to pay city, county or federal income taxes.

Things you should know:

Some states, (check your state to see), issue tax lien

certificates to the public. What happens is the city will determine what is owed to it, as far as taxes, interest and penalties. Then a tax lien certificate is issued based upon that. Tax lien options are held for anyone interested in buying Tax Lien Certificates. Study up on this investment opportunity. There are plenty of books on this information in circulation. As a purchaser of the tax lien certificates you pay whatever taxes interest and penalties that are attached to the lien if you secure the bid on it at the auction. In return you receive your principal investment back plus interest. Some states give 16% 18% even up to 24% interest. That's a serious return on your money!

Position yourself to purchase the property if the tax lien holder does not pay up. Even though this book is not about Tax Lien Certificates, I strongly suggest that you learn about the investment side of it. If you decide to get really serious about investing in real estate. Why, because this is another real estate grind where you can make money no matter which way the coin flips. Either you are going to receive your investment dollars back plus interest, or you are going to be given the opportunity to take ownership of the property. If the property owners don't redeem the property. If you go out and purchase a book on investing in Tax Lien Certificates, you will still be consistent with investing in inner city properties. Many of the tax lien certificate properties are located in the urban communities, and if you have never before heard of tax lien certificates investing until purchasing this book, that means you are out of the loop in terms of the real estate investment opportunities around you.

Even some financial planners and money managers have failed to fulfill their obligation of informing their clients of these types of investment opportunities. Lack of education and awareness, in financial investment matters, breeds dependency on others! The Internet is a wealth of information, so tap into it. And if you don't know how to navigate through the Internet learn how. Now here's another point I wanted to mention about the tax lien placed on inner city physically distressed properties.

In some cities the local government policies are nonprofit organization friendly. By that I mean the administration will give preferential treatment and allow the nonprofit organizations to take the tax delinquent properties off their books once the city forecloses on it. This is why a lot of housing based nonprofit organizations have been formed in most cities. Some of these organizations sole purpose is to assist and meet the demand of affordable housing because in actuality, the board of directors know that the Real Estate Grind is the Inner Cities goldmine. They are just working the grind! While satisfying a burgeoning need. These people, (board of directors) that run these organizations have identified a housing need and have found a vehicle to supply that need. So why not join them!

Author's Thoughts: The urban communities are so saturated with distressed properties that it's like having more than enough food on one plate. Everybody can eat off of the same plate!

10 Becoming an Owner Occupant

Owner occupant what does it mean? An owner occupant is someone not only who owns the property, but they reside there as well.

Once you become a property owner, whether by yourself or through a shared equity partnership, or some other type. If you are receiving government assistance it changes your social status at least in part, and therefore you have a legal obligation to notify your caseworker. In such cases, expect to have your government assistance discontinued, and please do not be discouraged by this information. You can look at this opportunity as a way of beginning the process of economic independence. After speaking with an attorney acquaintance of mine who has handled this type of situation, he stated to me that typically when a person purchases property if they are currently receiving government aid, all their benefits will be cut off!

He stated that the Only exception was when the property was gifted to the individual, or it was received by way of a will or trust. (Talk to an attorney to see if this law still exists). So, if you are a recipient of government subsidies, money, food stamps rental assistance etc., and you buy an investment property, you are required by law to notify your caseworker. Failure to do so will result in the loss of all government aid, and restitution reimbursement of funds determined by the welfare agency, and possible fraud charges brought against you resulting in incarceration or probation. This is why it is vitally important for you to understand and weigh out the challenges of buying investment property if you are presently on welfare.

Obviously if you're not a welfare recipient, you don't have to concern yourself with any type of government reprisal, or action taken against you that could be harmful. But in the case where you will be occupying one of the units in the property, make sure you crunch your numbers in terms of what utilities you will have to pay (property taxes, insurance, and maintenance of the property), how much rent you will be receiving ,and will the rental income from the other units be enough to carry the property without it being a financial burden to you. By having someone in your team (real estate attorney) that can put together a pro forma statement, you can create a financial picture of the property's income potential. The word pro forma means As If in Latin. And what this actually means is when a pro forma statement is created on a prospective property, each expense amount and rental income assigned dollar amount represents the As If. The scenario that follows is given to help you understand the pro forma concept:

You have found a property that you have already qualified, and you are now valuing. The depreciated value accumulation is a valuation method you use to determine what the property is worth to you in its current condition. If you want to take it a step further and give the property some numbers as if it was already up and running the pro forma statement should be your means of choice.

OK, so you have found a two-family property with two bedrooms on each floor, and you checked with Section 8 and found out that they pay $850 for two bedrooms. The property has separate utilities so that means each tenant will be responsible for paying their electric and gas. As a landlord you know that you will be paying the water and sewer, property taxes, insurance, as well as your own electric and gas. Ideally you want the rental income produced from the unit you're going to rent out to pay for all of your annual expenses. The pro forma statement will give you an indication of if you should expect a rental income shortfall. So, after calling around to various servicing agencies you were able to collect the information needed to aid you, and the format below represents the financial picture of all the gathered information.

Pro Forma Statement

Gross potential annual income: $10,200

Vacancy Allowance: 0 renting out to Section8

Gross Annual Operating Income: $10,200

Utilities Annual Operating Expense

Electric $150 -this figure represents your monthly electric bill for the apartment you're living in.
Gas $150 -this figure represents your monthly gas bill for the apartment you're living in.
Sewer/Water $125 -this is a monthly figure.
Heat/Oil $3000 -this is a landlord bill you will only have to be concerned with approximately 6 1/2 months out of the year.
Insurance $50 -this is a monthly bill you pay.
Property taxes $1500 -you pay this bill once a year
Maintenance $250 -this figure will vary but it shouldn't be high.
Total Operating Expenses: $5225

$10200 (Gross annual potential income)
-$5225 (Annual operating expenses)
$4975

Now let's average the $4975 out monthly. 4975 divided by 12 = 414.58
So based upon the monthly rental income average you should have a positive monthly cash flow of $414.58.
Again, this above listed number projection is dependent on the figures stated remaining consistent, but it gives you a clear mental picture of what your financial reality can be providing the numbers remain consistent.

For safe practices I would suggest that you create at least a $200 to $600 margin of error, because with rental income numbers like the ones in this scenario, you definitely have to remain conscious. Don't forget that upon purchasing the property because you use the Property Equity Niche Investment Approach, you inherited a significant amount of property equity, just sitting and waiting for you to access it once you're ready! Because people's financial conditions vary, each interested real estate investor is going to have to evaluate their situation first. Then make a decision on if the time is best for them to get involved with the real estate investment grind. Also, remember that if the income the property produces is not federally taxed, it will probably be taxed by the state or the local area you reside in. This is an issue for your tax expert to examine for you.

Author Thoughts: human life is made up of a transitional process. From the time of conception, we go from an embryo to a fetus to an infant, to a little child, to a teenager, to adulthood. This evolutionary development is governed by a biological order. By the same token, mental growth and development is also a process which is governed by what information we receive. It's relevant to our interpretations of it, and how we ultimately apply it. If we don't have a full understanding of it, the likelihood of misapplying it becomes great! Hence, this book's chapter composition. Like the other chapters in this book is to help you see and understand the process of being an owner occupant. Always, I repeat, always carry out your numbers crunching process, which is your due diligence. Just like in this chapter, so that you don't get blindsided after the fact with a negative cash flow situation.

11 An Idea on How to Hold Your Property

In chapter 4, Raising Private Capital Through a Partnership, we covered the reason why you want to form a real estate partnership. In that chapter the shared equity partnership was used for illustration purposes. But I'd like to state that the shared equity partnership does not give you the personal liability you need. Please seek legal representation on this issue. The partnership serves as an instrument to reflect what the partnership is made of. In terms of the duration of the partnership, who the members are, who are the financial contributors, how much investment capital was contributed per member, who the decision makers of the partnership are, how the equity profits from the property are going to be distributed amongst the partners, and how the tax liability will affect each partner.

However, in this chapter the focus is going to be on protecting yourself from a personal liability court judgment that could possibly relegate you to a wretched life of poverty. Real estate beginners should seriously consider holding their properties as a limited liability company. If their attorney advises you to do so, do it. Let's look at what limited liability is. Limited Liability is the restriction of one's potential loss to the amount of investment. What this means is if a partnership was formed and it was structured to protect certain partners, then the only loss they would be exposed to is their initial capital investment.

What is a limited liability company? Limited liability company, LLC, is a cross between a corporation and a partnership, the limited liability company must be created by documents filed in the same place of incorporation.

Author Thoughts: the real estate grind is more about one's mental acumen, clearness of vision, than physical ability, because it is based on possessing or developing something not everyone has, discipline, skill and vision. The real estate investment grind is about making money with your Mind not your physical skills!

12 Determining the Return on Your Investment Dollars

OK so your property has been restored, your tenants have been paying rent for one year now, and so it's time to figure out how your investment dollars have performed! This chapter deals with an easy number crunching system. In this chapter you will learn what your Capital investment means, how to figure out what the return is, and what the term net operating income or NOI is.

Now let's get started.

What is your capital investment? Simply put, your capital investment is the cash you use in the purchasing of all costs associated with this process and restoring of the property. Remember you purchased all of your properties with cash. The Capital investment return is an annual, (end of the year), rate of return that is expressed in two different forms. It is expressed as a dollar amount, and it is expressed as a percentage.

Net operating income. Income from the property after operating expenses have been deducted but before paying your taxes. In the case of a property investment owner the NOI is what is left over after he has paid the property taxes, heat oil, insurance, utilities, repairs, property management fees, maintenance etc.

After he pays all of those expenses, or whatever expenses he is responsible for paying, throughout the year, his net operating income is what's left. But this is not his Net income, what is left after federal and state taxes.

Now here is the scenario I want to walk you through. You have a two-family unit that you purchased for $20,000 and restored for $5000. It has 2 bedrooms on each floor that you're receiving $750 dollars per unit a month for. It also has separate utilities, (meaning that the tenant pays utilities, electric and gas.) Your total capital investment into the property is $25,000. This form below is for illustration purposes only.

I would suggest that if you're going to commit to operating as a Property Equity Niche Investor, you should learn how to prepare this type of forma, or at least have someone on your team that. The format is called an Annual Property Operating Data, also known as APOD.

Gross Scheduled Income: $18,000 (total rental income received for the year.) Other Income: $0, (This would be income if you had coin operated washers, and dyers installed in the basement or if you were renting out a garage.)

Vacancy allowance $0 (If you're renting out to Section8, vacancy should not be an issue. When it comes to the issue of Vacancy Allowance, conventional wisdom suggests that you use a 10% Vacancy Allowance rate. That way loss of rent is factored in, giving you a safety net, as well as an idea of what your rental income picture would look like should you have any Vacancy.

Gross Operating Income: $18000

Operating Expenses:

Electric $0

Gas $0

Sewer $700

Water $800

Heat/Oil $2000

Insurance $ 1200

Property Taxes $1800

Maintenance $ 250

Total operating expense: $6,750

Gross operating income, minus operating expenses represents your Net Operating Income.

Remember this dollar amount is before you pay your federal and state taxes. Your tax expert will help you with determining your Net Income What's left after paying your Federal and state taxes) in each property you own. Now we see the need to express the Net Operating Income (11,250) as a percentage, and this is achieved by dividing the net operating income 11,250 by your capital investment, 25000, then multiplying the two figures by 100%. For instance,

$11250 45% This is what it looks like in a ratio and proportion format.

$25000 100%

Here's another way to look at it. $ 11,250 divided by $25,00. = A 45 % return on your Capital Investment.

A 45% return on your Capital Investments, even though it's a before tax rate of return, it's quite impressive in real estate. Don't discount the other factors you have in your favor. What's that you ask? Well, if you recall you purchased the property for cash, (See Chapter 9) using the Property Equity Niche Investor

Approach, correct?

Then you should have a significant amount of equity in the property, because there are no liens on your property. And you purchased it well below its "as is repaired" market value. There are no monthly payments for you to make. Once you become more efficient in the real estate grind, you can borrow against the equity in your investment property and purchase other physically distressed neighborhood properties using this same system. This system of investing in real estate allows you to legally turn your money without a high degree of financial risk. You just find, purchase, rehab, rent out (or resell) and watch the Gold Nuggets come flowing in.

In this grind, there's no fighting or arguing about your money because the government pays the lion share (the majority of what's owed to you) and in some cases, all of the rent. The affordable housing need is real and it's very lucrative. The Department of Housing and Urban Development, Section 8, rental assistance program is the program you want to target as a real estate Property Equity Niche Investor. The local Housing Authority in charge of overseeing this program will gladly pay you on time for helping it accommodate this pressing housing rental issue.

In the illustration shown to you the Part is $11,250 and the Whole is $25,000.

<u>Part $11,250 = ?</u> You are solving for the percentage of the whole number
Whole $25,000 = 100 that's why the question mark is there.

It's like someone saying to you $11,250 is what percent of $25,000? As you see the part $11,250 represents a percentage of the whole number $25,000. In this case the part represents the net operating income and also the return on your capital investment period. The line that separates the two numbers above tells you that operation of division is to be used. Don't forget, this is a two-step process which consists of division and multiplication. So now let's solve the equation by determining what percentage $11,250 represents of $25,000.

$11,250 divided by $25,000 x 100% = 45%. $11,250 represents 45% of $25,000. Now you can take the time out to process this mathematical equation with a calculator. Congratulations, I'm sure your answer was 45%. It's just that simple. The Return on Investment or ROI is 45%. If this entire process was written out in explanation form, it would read as follows: when you're trying to figure out what the return on your capital investment is, you take the net operating income divided by your capital investment and multiply it by 100%. The reason why you multiply the numbers by 100% is so the decimal place will be in its proper place on the right side of the quotient, (the answer) instead of the left side.

Author's Thoughts. Your money is like your personal soldiers who you send out on a recruitment mission. It is the job of your money to go forth on a recruitment mission and bring back exponentially (increase in large amounts) more of its kind. You shouldn't be working for your money all of your life, at some point, your money should be working for you! The real estate grind allows you to get the most satisfying production for your time, energy, commitment and money.

13 Becoming a Real Estate Professional

Now that you have chosen the real estate rental business as your grind, you will at some point be designated as a real estate professional/dealer. In this chapter you will be provided with the definition of what a real estate professional is based upon the Internal Revenue Service criteria. The following information has been taken from publication 527, titled residential rental property. You can obtain a copy for free of the entire publication by contacting the IRS.

Real estate professional. If you meet the qualifications covered in the following text, you have to report your rental income on schedule C or C-EZ. (You can also use 1065 if you're holding the property as a partnership.) again seek legal assistance in this matter. The information given here is just to remind you of the importance of performing your due diligence. You qualify as a real estate professional for the tax year if you meet both of the following requirements:

-More than half of the personal services you perform in all trades or businesses during the tax year are performed as real property trades or businesses in which you materially participated as a landlord. Or

- You perform more than 750 hours of services during the tax year in real property real estate trades or businesses in which you materially participate. Material participation for you is handling any of the responsibilities that come along with being a landlord. For purposes of meeting these qualifications each interest(investment) in real estate is a separate activity unless you elect to treat all your interest in rental real estate as one activity.

What qualifies as real property trades or businesses? A real property trade or business is a trade or business that does any of the following with real property:

- Develops or re-develops it
- Constructs or reconstructs it
- Acquires it
- Converts it if you get involved with single room occupancy conversions
- Rents or leases it.
- Operates or manages it.
- Or broker it.

A broker is a state licensed agent who charges a fee in handling the transactions between property owners or buyers in real estate transactions. You can choose to treat all interest, (property investments) as due activity. If you were a real estate professional and had more than one rental real estate interest during the year you can choose to treat all the interest as one activity. You can make this choice for any year that you qualify as a real estate professional. If you forgo on making the choice for one year, you can still make it for a later year. All of this is a process that you would sit down with your real estate tax attorney and have him explain to you.

If you make the choice to treat all the interest as one activity it is binding for the tax year. You are a real estate professional. Again, this is an issue for you and your real estate tax attorney to discuss. I have included this information on being a real estate professional for your knowledge and awareness of what favorable classifications the IRS gives to those that meet the housing need in America.

To qualify as a real estate professional in terms of hours is 750 hours of real estate involvement, as a property investor or landlord. Which includes riding around towns looking for property, qualifying the property, searching property records, performing the tenant selection process or overseeing the rehabilitation process etc. In fact, in one year you can be considered a real estate professional if you just worked two hours and 10 minutes a day for one year. Focus your attention on this. There are 365 days in a year and all you need to do is devote 750 hours towards real estate activities to qualify as a professional. Well, here's the mathematical equation on how you would figure out how many hours you needed to work a day to satisfy the 750 hours standard. If you divided 750 into 365 days. Your answer would be 748.25 days for one year. But if you spend 2 hours and 6 minutes a day for the year it would give you 751.9 hours to your credit for the year. Remember you only need 750 hours to become a real estate professional (As of this written).

There's also plenty of tax advantages that the real estate professional status will afford you. Make sure you discuss these tax advantages with your tax expert. You need to know all about the preferential tax treatment you will receive as a landlord. I hope at this point in the book your perspective is clearer, and you can see why there's no better grind for you than the real estate grind!

Author's Thoughts: Taxation plays a major role in the way the financially educated ones invest their money. That's why when you hear or read about where they put their money. If you doubt what I'm saying, find some time to look at the richest people in the Word, and then do a Google search on their holdings. You will see that the common thread that links them all together is that they are heavily invested in real estate. You see, they already know what I'm trying to help you see. It's now time for you to get in on the action. Stop standing on the sideline and get into the real estate grind business!

14 The Business of Apartment Rentals

Apartment rental is a business within itself. In the business world you have the products, the services and the consumers. The real estate grind is governed by these same elements. Did you know that your spending habits are studied, recorded and reflected by what is known as the Consumer Price Index? The services and products that you buy are closely monitored. Your spending patterns are studied, and then these specific markets, where the index shows you spend most of your hard-earned dollars, are aggressively advertised. What is the definition of the consumer price index?.

Consumer Price Index. The most widely known of many such measures of price levels and inflation that are reported to the US government. It measures and compares from month to month the total cost of a statistically determined market basket of goods and services consumed by U.S. households.

In the beginning of this chapter, I mention three different elements that make up the business world: products, services, and the consumers. In the same breath I showed you how it's relative to you as a landlord, by what products and services you provide, and who the consumers are. If you now view the same different elements from the standpoint of a landlord, you can see how it relates to apartments being rented out as a business. To make my point clearer, all you have to do is look at the affordable housing demand in the area you reside in. If you do, you will notice that the demand for affordable housing exceeds the supply of available housing. This is why The Real Estate Grind Is the Inner City's Gold Mine!

The monthly cash flow provided to you from the property

can really start to change your financial situation gradually. It's all about providing a good product and service (a habitable residence) to your renter. With some of the rental income you can start paying down some of your bills, in particular credit card debt, as well as look to reinvest some money in some other income producing venture. I understand that because everyone's financial picture is not the same, everyone's road map to being financially secure will be different. However, the point I'm simply trying to make here is that the Apartment Rental Business is a great place to start building generational wealth!

Basic business principles dictate that in order to realize a profit in whatever business you are in, you need to make sure that most of the money that comes in stays in! Your property expenses and personal monthly debt payment Can't be more than what the property is producing as income. If it is, you are dealing with a negative cash flow, and you need to reassess that situation to see where you get rid of, or to reduce your monthly debt. Your net rental income profit is not what you make, it's what you keep. Please remember that!

Author's thoughts: a lot of us, including myself, have been poor Stewart's or Keepers in the way we have managed our money and either bills (a form of debt) or credit given to us by creditors (i.e,the appliance stores, department stores, Furniture Merchants Banks and other credit card issuers). We are drowning in some form of debt. Every company that extends their credit services to us knows this! If you only knew how much interest you pay on credit given to you, you probably would never again utilize credit. At least not for debt purposes only! We have become a society enslaved by credit and debt owed to others. And the only winners are the ones that money is owed. Even when a landlord rents out an apartment to someone, it's a form of credit because they're banking on you paying your rent on time in the future. This is why a lot of times they run your credit first (using a rental application form). It's to determine your ability to pay your rent in the future. Like I said previously, it's all about who owes whom in a capitalistic society. This is what it means when you hear a person in despair say", I'm working hard just to pay off my credit cards or other forms of debt.". I encourage all of my readers to find a way to position yourself whereby you can reap the benefits from this Debt Owed system we all are a part of. The time has come to free yourself from this bondage!

15 The Section 8 Landlord Application Process

This chapter is an informational one that contains the landlord application process, compliments of various eHow website contributors. I included this information to help you better understand what this process consists of so that you can effectively prepare for it. The process is for the most part uniform without any regard to the state you live in because it is mostly established by federal laws and regulations. However, there may be a slight variation in some states based on jurisdictional discretion, exercised by that state Housing Authority agent. Your real estate attorney, as well as a housing agency staff member will guide you through the entire process to make sure that you meet the Housing Authority Section 8 landlord requirements. See Appendix 2

Single Room Occupancy (S.R.O)

Now here's one of the exciting subjects every right investor enjoys experiencing. The focus in this chapter is on maximizing your gross annual rental income, using the Single Room Occupancy, AKA Rooming House conversion approach. First you need to know what a single room occupancy, SRO, Rooming House is. A Single room Occupancy is a type of housing in which residents have a private bedroom, but share other areas such as the kitchen, bathroom, living room or entertainment area. Typically, these are created for very low-income housing and elderly housing. Which is Section 8 type of housing programs. Where I am from, there are housing arrangements like this available to those individuals living with AIDS as well. If you reside in an urban community that has a combination of single-family houses, two family, or 3 family houses, your chances of the city you're from allowing you to convert the property into a rooming house AKA single room occupancy are good.

For your mental Clarity I have to take the initiative to present to you two separate illustrations, classified as scenario number one and scenario number two. These will show you what your gross annual rental income would be as a result of renting it out as an apartment, and then renting it out as a single room occupancy rooming house.

Exceptions to the Property Equity Niche Investment Approach: if you have the opportunity to purchase a single-family distress house and know beforehand that you will be able to convert it into a single room occupancy house, then buy it. Because the conversion will produce enough rental income to make the investment an economically sound one.

Caution: If you can't convert it don't purchase it!

Single room occupancy rooming housing conversion maximizing your properties rental income:

Scenario#1This scenario begins after Renovations have been performed and the property is being rented out.

- Property address: 415 Park Street San Diego California
- Property type: Two family unit
- Section 8 paying $700 for each unit.
- Rooms per unit: 2 bedrooms, living room, kitchen, bathroom
- Separate Utilities
- Owner pays sewer, water, property taxes, insurance
- Tenant pays electric, gas, heat

- Each unit is being rented out for $700.

$700 x 2 = $1,400 oh, this is your gross monthly income times 12 months which equals $16,800. This figure represents your gross annual rental income

Your annual operating expenses:

Utilities: sewer $200, water $375, insurance $1800, repairs and maintenance $150, property taxes $1,850 and miscellaneous $75.

Total annual expenses $4,125

Total annual rental income $16,800

Net operating income $12,675

Scenario #2:

Now, let's look at the scenario from a single room occupancy perspective. Property address 415 Park Street San Diego California property type: Two family unit. After purchasing the property, you decide to turn it into a Single Room Occupancy to maximize the rental income. So, the first thing you do is obtain the necessary paperwork from the building code Department. See the Business License application, building permit form, from the city I'm from at the end of the chapter. Note: once you receive approval to convert the property into a rooming house, your property will be classified as a business!

You will also be instructed on what conversion work needs to be done in order to be in compliance with the building code and the necessary building permits. Okay you received approval from your city building department to proceed. Your contractor starts the conversion process and finishes It 2 months later. The property has now been converted into 8 bedrooms. The city building inspector comes out, and inspects the job, and grants you the Certificate of Occupancy.

Now you can contact the Housing Authority Section 8 Department and inform them of your decision to be a Section 8 housing single room occupancy provider. They will more than likely also provide you with paperwork to fill out, and at such time you can inquire about what section 8 pays a week. Yes, that's right. You will receive weekly rental payments as a rooming housing operator.

Note. And each state the weekly rental payment may vary. Whatever Section 8 pays weekly should be documented and you should be provided with this information once you serve notice About wanting to be involved in the section 8 rental housing provider program. In this scenario you will receive $90 a week. Now the exciting phase kicks in when determining how much guaranteed money you will receive every week.

Investor beware: a word of caution using this method will increase your utility bill and other operating expenses associated with the business operation of the property. You should still have a positive cash flow left after all of your financial obligations are met. Here is what the numbers for this scenario look like.

There are 8 bedrooms. Each room is being rented out for $90. $90 X 8 x 4 equals $2,880 a month.

Now, let’s look at it from a gross annual rental income viewpoint.

90x8x4x12=$ 34,560

The $2,880 represents the gross monthly income from the

property. The $34,560 represents the annual income from the property. Now let's develop the scenario a little more by adding the annual operating expenses.

Owner's Annual Operating Expenses:

Utilities

Electric $3250

Water $500

Sewer $450

Heat/Oil $3500

Other Expenses:

Property Taxes $1800

Insurance $1500

Repairs and maintenance $1500, (this number should be low due to conversion and repair work done the 1st year).

Miscellaneous $75

Total Annual Expenses: $15325

Total Gross Annual Rental Income: $34560

Minus

Total Annual Operating Expenses: $15,325

$19,235 this is the net operating income

By converting this property into a single room occupancy

rooming house, you increased the net operating income by $6,560 or 51.76%, in comparison to scenario number one $12,675 net operating income. I know you're probably saying at this point where I get this above stated figure from. Well remember, in scenario number one, we looked at what the properties maximum gross rental income potential would be by renting out the apartments. And in that scenario the net operating income was $12,675. By contrast in this scenario, you converted the property into a single room occupancy, and by doing so, you increased the net operating income by 65.8%.

So, the question Still Remains how did I get this percentage? Here's how you would mathematically process this situation. Step one, you take the net operating income of $19,235 from Scenario number two and subtract from the net operating income of scenario number one $12,675. The difference between the two figures is $6,560. Now you set up a ratio formatted as follow.

$6,560 divided by $ 12,675 x 100% = 51.7%

The $12,675 is the whole number because it represents the first source of income, when determining how much of a percentage and dollar amount increase between the two scenarios, because it was the first figure to be established in the scenario sequence. So when you compare the two figures, and each scenario, the $12,675 takes the position of the whole number and is lined up with the 100 % under the division line, and the figure representing the part is placed above the division line because it is a percentage of the whole number.

Do you remember how to solve for the unknown

percentage? This was covered in chapter 11. We'll just in case you can't remember here is the process. $6,560 divided by $12,675 Times 100% equals 51.76%. This is a two-step process that you must commit to memory. The single room occupancy AKA Rooming House conversion approach is your architectural design or blueprint to maximizing the annual revenue that your property business will be generating.

Note: Going this route enables you to create a strong weekly cash flow. You paid cash for the property so there's no monthly mortgage payments to make. The government subsidy housing program Section 8 pays the utilities for you through the check you will be receiving weekly/monthly. And because you purchased the property in a distressed state, you have a significant amount of equity in the property available for you to borrow against anytime you're ready!

Author's Thoughts: This book is my platform to communicate to those of you in the inner cities the vital importance of not only working up and smelling the coffee, but also tasting it, so you can experience its goodness! I don't want you to just be a witness of someone else's economic progress. I want you to be a partaker of your own economic success. You have been consigned to a life of Real Estate disenfranchisement long enough, through some traditional lending Institutions (and to date, we are still faced with challenges when it comes to accessing lending institutions capital). You are an urban community resident who has just as much right to the same investment opportunities within your community, as those that live outside of the community. This is why this book is so timely. It is now time for you to get the ball rolling. I have consciously chosen to expose you. To a more safe and financially attainable

Grind to get you started.

This book is about challenging you to step out of the boat and into the shallow end of the water first, then you can decide when you are ready for the deep end, the more advanced real estate grind!

16 Marketing Your Product

This chapter begins by establishing what your product is. As discussed previously your product is the apartment you provide to the renters of this world. What is a market?

1. A gathering of people buying and selling things.
2. An open space or building where goods are shown for sale.
3. A shop for the sale of provisions such as a meat market.
4. A region in which Goods can be bought and sold. European market
5. Trade: buying and selling
6. Demand: As in a demand for Housing.

Businesses that offer products or Services devote a significant amount of money towards Marketing. In fact, before the start of any business, one must take into account the market they're going to Target, and how much money they can afford to spend in it. At this juncture in the book, I am hoping that you realize the power of, and the beauty in the Property Equity Niche Investment Approach.

The sixth definition of the word market is the man. And in that context, what it means is that there are a percentage of people in Need or Want of something in particular (and in this case, the affordable housing market). The law of Supply and Demand is a fundamental economic concept, which holds that the price (in this case rent) is set at an amount where the quantity (amount) of housing supplied, and the quantity (amount of housing) that's in demand are addressed.

Example: If there are more apartment rentals than needed by

renters, the rents charged will have to be reduced to a lower amount. By contrast, when there are more renters than available apartment rentals, the rent charged to the renters will be upwardly adjusted. After reading this book, do your own research and you will discover that the market demand for affordable housing in the United States is uncontainable. All you have to do is check with your local housing authority, and this undeniable fact will be confirmed! Now back to the Property Equity Niche Investment Approach. The government sponsored Section 8 program is the meal ticket for you and your family. Because the reality is that there will always be a segment of society who will be in need of government housing subsidy support. Which means that if you decide that the real estate apartment rental business is for you, you will not have to be concerned with the burdensome market costs.

One of your marketing approaches will be to contact your local housing authority Section 8 department, and formally notify the person in charge, and express your wish to be placed on the affordable housing provider list as a landlord. They will then provide you with the necessary documents to qualify. Think about this for a moment. There is already a pre-established affordable housing rental market. All you have to be willing to do is Supply it!

Author's Thought: I want for you to have your fair share of the American pie, by enjoying the financial comfortability You are entitled to, but I can't want it more for you than you want it for yourself.

17 Advertising Your Apartment Rental Business

In this chapter we are going to take a more in depth look at your biggest Advertiser. The local Housing Authority. Okay, so now you're open for business but how do you inform your target market of it? Through advertisements of course.

Advertisement is a very important tool to use and in addition to going through the housing authority, landlords also will take out an ad in the local newspaper classified section (for a fee). And depending on how long they have to run the ad to find a tenant, maintaining the ad space can be costly. But the distinct(clear) advantage you have by using the housing authority to do your advertising is that none of your money is depleted (used up) in advertisement costs. Once you file with them, they will advertise for you. How terrific is that!

Once your renovations are done, the required housing forms filled out, and your tenants in place, the real estate grind system covered in this book will enable you to operate your apartment rental business smoothly. And guess what? Whenever a housing related issue does occur, you already have a team of professionals to address it. All the headaches that could occur are shifted to one of your team members certified to deal with such matters.

Advertisement is only effective if it creates the environment of awareness and interest expected. If you are unsuccessful in doing this, those invested dollars are wasted, and your hopes of being a prosperous businessperson may not be as promising as you thought it would be! I remember when I was producing a show at a social hall, I rented it out in the month of July. The only advertisement I did was printing up the flyers, passing it out, and posting it up in different businesses, using the word-of-mouth advertisement approach. I charged a reasonable admission fee at the door. I went out and brought all this food (which was free to those that attended). I also purchased (for sale) whiskey, champagne and beer. I also paid for the live entertainment I offered. And guess what? It flopped! Smh. I did not make back anywhere near what it cost me to provide the entertainment. After the show I still had a lot of whiskey, champagne and beer left but no food was left (no surprise there). Luckily it was during the summertime. So, I decided to go to the local park and sell what was left. But the question becomes why it was a flop!

Two reasons, Marketing and Advertising. I did not adhere (follow) the principles that govern each one. I presumed that because I had the money, rented out the venue, reasonably priced the admission fee, printed up and passed out the flyers, in businesses that had a high level of foot traffic, told mostly everyone I knew, and above all, provided a form of entertainment (that typically produces profit) it would be a success but unfortunately, it wasn't. After the show, the manager of the group I brought in from New York approached me and explained to me where I went wrong. He said that I produced a show (of that nature) during a time when people had a million other things they could be entertained by (intense competition and not enough demand). He told me "We will come back in the winter, when the demand is high to be entertained, and pack this place". My response was "let's do it".

Had I done a market analysis, I would have learned that Summertime is not the best time to produce a show like the one I was offering. What I should've done was started advertising the show in the Summer, that would be taking place in the Winter.

That would've given me 5 months of advertisement. But you, on the other hand, do not have to worry about the marketing or the advertisement of your apartment rental business because it has already been taken care of for you, by the local housing authority. The product and services you're offering as a landlord meets the increasing demand. In fact, just the other day, I was given an article about the mortgage crisis, and it stated that (In the bad neighborhoods, there's a great deal of blighted boarded up houses. Now when you see or even hear something like that, what should it mean to you? That's a gold mine opportunity for you. I hope by now you're starting to see the picture more clearly!

Each Section8 approved individual receives a housing provider list. So don't be surprised when you call about one of your apartments for rent. Once you screen them and approve their application, it's a wrap. This is a sweet grind, when you stick to the system, I'm sharing with you.

Author's Thought: Oftentimes in life, we make a simple journey a lot more difficult than it actually has to be. That's why when I discuss the real estate grind with people, I explain to them that the best path to explore for a novice(beginner), as a real estate investor, is the path of least resistance. I have consciously gone to great lengths in this book to reveal to you this path, through a system that has proven to be extremely efficient for those of you that are committed and confident enough to try it. The Property Equity Niche Investment Approach discussed in this book, is a systematic approach to accessing the gold that each distressed property in the inner city possesses.

18 Making Sure Your Property/ies Are Properly Managed

Property Management is not all that challenging as the sound of it may suggest. The key to effective property management lies in a single word "Delegation". Check out the Webster Dictionary definition of the word. Delegation- 1. A person authorized to act for others. 2. To entrust (authority) to another. It's all about giving out assignments to different people, to handle different property related responsibilities.

The following listed professionals will be responsible for handling all your property related issues:

1. Electrician. Any electric issue will be addressed by this person
2. Carpenter. All carpentry work needed will be performed by this person.
3. Maintenance Worker/Superintendent. You will need someone to handle the upkeep (e.g., cutting the grass, removal of livestock).
4. Lawyer. To handle property related tenant and landlord issue, or any other legal issues that may arise concerning the property.
5. Accountant. You will definitely need an accountant for the preparation of your taxes.
6. Painter. For the obvious

You as a landlord have to be willing to appoint qualified individuals to carry out the above-stated responsibilities. Family, personal time, peace of mind and the ability to be in the field pre-qualifying other investments properties is something that all real estate investors value. Therefore, it is essential that a property management team be assembled at some point. Since you do not want to receive calls at all times of the night, it would be best to provide your tenants with the name and phone number of your superintendent. Inform them that in case of any property related repairs, they should contact him/ her. And do the same for your superintendent.

Some people may take the position that just starting out, and having only one property, does not require having a property management team. And if you concur (agree), then you need to ask yourself, what type of repairs am I qualified to perform in the event of a repair or replace situation? Once the restoration process has occurred, and you've rented your property out. Repairs or replacements of the property will be any issue for a while. I'm so excited for you about the range of possibilities that real estate offers, on so many different levels, and I know that many of you will be successful after studying, and then practicing the investment principles in this book.

As you can now see that property management isn't about the intense, unrelenting labor for you as a landlord. It's about the organizational skills you possess or are willing to learn! Management without organization is much like having a bell installed at your home that does not work. It's all symbols without substance! These two go hand in hand. Here's why I say this. If you say as a New Year's resolution That you are going to start working out more. Then along with that commitment normally comes a dietary schedule, a daily workout schedule, and what part of the body you're going to work on throughout the week. Let's say you are going to work out Monday through Friday and rest on the weekends. Then you decide that you will eat breakfast at 5:30, and then determine what each breakfast will be on Monday -Friday. This is organization but then you just have the follow through (commitment)to get it done. You can't have one without the other!

Author's Thought: I hope in this chapter I have been to you the beacon (light) that shows you that you do have an alternative route to the more popular one taken by the masses. Organizing a management team for your property(ies) can be a simple and effective way of land lording. As long as you have the proper system in place, your apartment rental business will flourish!

19 How to Form a Real Estate Investors Club

In the world of Poker, they have a saying which is called playing short stack. What it means is your poker chip count is low. So, if your funds are limited this chapter presents another way you can get in on the action! Now I'm going to inform you that I will not be dealing with every detail of forming a Real Estate Investment Club. I will leave that part for the experts on your team, the attorney and the accountant. What I will be speaking about is how you can use this investment vehicle to put some money in your pocket, as well as provide a way for the rest of the club members to increase their bottom line.

You will have to determine what the term (partnership longevity), as well as the terms (how much each member will contribute, and how the distribution system will work) of the real estate investment Club is going to be. Also remember that since you are the Visionary, you must take the lead on this. With the help of your attorney and accountant of course. You just need to explain to them what it is you want to do, and they will advise you on the best way to accomplish it. There are online websites that can also give your ideas. Research this first! You will have to find some people interested in investing, and then once you have their interest, you must be able to communicate your vision to them in a way that even a baby will understand. Hopefully they will respond by signing on as investors.

If they can mentally see what you see, they are more likely to get involved. By contrast people are less likely to get involved in anything they can't wrap their minds around! The better you understand it, the better you will be able to help someone else understand it! Having stated this, it is now time to take a closer look at what the Real Estate Investment Club is about. Gather some of the community residents you are close with and propose this idea to them. Hopefully they will see the wisdom, and what you want to do, and how they fit in. Ask them the question, "why should we allow someone outside of the community to buy the property we should be buying?" Because I know you (the reader) care about the people in the community in which you live, you (the reader) must be the one to take a proactive role in shaping and molding it (the community in which you live) into one that is safe, loving and reinforcing of the quality of life needed!

And after studying on the Property Equity Niche Investment Approach, you should thereafter be fully aware of the principle on how to execute it, and what the end results should be! Again, shop around the Real Estate Investment Club idea to different people, in the Inner City to create a buzz on what you are currently working on to put together. Obviously, this happens once you have obtained the knowledge and understanding necessary to organize this type of investment vehicle. Arrange for a meeting with parties interested on a particular day, and time and place. Then be prepared to lay out your investment plan strategy to them.

At the outset, explain to the interested parties the role you're going to take on, versus what each member role will be. Will you be the one to organize it and do the property pre-qualifying valuations and acquisitions? You will be the one to manage the ongoing affairs of the investment club property and, distribute the membership interest percentage of the profits. In other words, your contribution to the investment club can be the services you render, and you can take a percentage of the profits as monetary compensation such as a Management Fee.

Depending on your financial status, you may need a monthly income source to help you meet other financial obligations. You (and your accountant) will also have to consider your tax liability, as well as that of all the club members.

Here's an example to go along with the scenario. Let's say you put together a real estate investment Club of 10 people, including yourself. Each person will have a 10% interest in the investment club. You receive 10% interest in exchange for the services you provide in the form of a management fee. That would mean that you would be entitled to receive 10% of the investment club profits. If you elect to go with the above listed format, each member should be fully aware of the fact that the rents generated by the first property purchased, as well as any property equity borrowed against, will be reinvested for the purchasing of additional properties. But what happens if one of the club members is in need of some money? How are you going to handle that issue? You have to make allowances for that possibility.

Maybe you can lend it to them out of the investment club account. If you do just make sure that the investment club records reflect that. Your tax expert can address this question. There should be a treasurer to take care of the property generated funds. Someone you feel is trustworthy, personable, dependable, has good organization skills, and bookkeeping skills. They should also be someone you can work well with! Remember you are placing this person in a stewardship position (over the investment club funds), so they must possess the above-mentioned qualities. My motivation behind touching on this topic of a Real Estate Investment Club was not to stare you in that direction. All I wanted was merely to present you with information about the option you have in this real estate grind. If you are becoming more and more resolute (determined) about getting in on the action, consider this avenue. But only once you have thoroughly grasped the objective of this book's real estate investment approach. So, in light of this, I strongly suggest that if you're interested in using this capital raising method for real estate investment deals, you have to first gather all the data you can on it. In the meantime, focus on understanding the Property Equity Investment Approach, and apply its principles when seeking out investment opportunities.

Author's thoughts: As someone who has taken on the responsibility of showing you why the Real Estate Grind is truly the Inner City's Goldmine, I find myself struggling with the inclination to introduce to you the more advanced investment angles that can be put to work, ushering you into the land of the real estate Giants. But such an undertaking would undermine the reading behind this book's production. I have to remain cognizant(aware) of the fact that this book is about bringing you slowly into the real estate investment fold, on a beginner's level. If I should ever decide to produce a Real Estate Grind Part 2, for the more advanced real estate investor, I will certainly cover the inner workings of the various niche property markets that the heavyweights of the real estate grind engage in. By that time those of you who have been applying the Property Equity Niche Investment approach in the real estate branch of the apartment rental business, you will be ready for this next level of the real estate grind. Remember, if the mind can conceive it, and the heart can receive it, then the individual can achieve it!

20 Alligator or Goldmine?

In real estate terms an Alligator means a piece of property that you have to continuously feed, put money into, for various reasons. Its appetite is insatiable, (incapable of being satisfied). This is every Real Estate Investors nightmare. The term Alligator comes from purchasing a property that you have to constantly spend money on Because of its appetite. Obviously, by contrast the term Goldmine in real estate language means the property is like the United States of America Treasury Department to investors in that the constant flow of weekly or monthly rental income makes it a Money Printing Machine. Let's first look at what can be a property Alligator.

Scenario #1 Bill fits the profile of a conventional investor that invests in real estate for appreciation. When the property appreciates, Bill will refinance the property to pull out some equity in the property to invest in other property. At this point in the book, you should remember what the word refinance means. But just in case you forgot, refinance means to replace an old loan with a new loan. Bill finds property in Westport, Connecticut. It's a two-family and the asking price is $210,000. Bill gets on the phone and calls his realtor for a sale comparable analysis. He asked two questions. How much did the last two-family houses sell for in the area he's looking in? What is the appreciation rate in that particular area?

His realtor tells him that properties in the area are appreciating at 10%, and the last two-family houses sold last month for 225 thousand dollars, and it was located two blocks down from the property Bill is considering buying. No appraisal was done. He relied on the Sales Comparison Analysis but what caused the property to appreciate?

Causes of appreciation:

- Inflation
- Housing demand in a particular area as a result of low interest rates
- Additional improvements and developments in close proximity

In this case there is a high demand to move into the area Bill is targeting. So, he responds swiftly, and offers to purchase the property for the asking price of $210,000. Now in Bill's mind, since the last 2 family houses sold for $225,000, and if the properties in the area he's looking in are appreciating it 10%, that would make this two family house he's looking at worth approximately 230 $100,000, once the appreciation factor kicks in.

Bill is willing to put out 20% of the asking price as a down payment on the property. That will be $42,000. He will be seeking conventional financing of 80% of the asking price or 168,000. Conventional financing means you will be asking a lender to loan you 80% of the asking price. $168,000 + $42,000 equals the asking price of 210 thousand dollars. The lender agrees to loan Bill 168,000, at a fixed interest rate of 6% for 30 years.

Investor's Note: The longer the pay off period the less your monthly mortgage payments will be.

$168,000 at 6% for 30 years makes your monthly mortgage payment $1007.33. This example is just for illustration purposes only!

Note: The lender uses what is called Amortization Chart to determine what the monthly payments will be for the borrower.

The loan principal amount is 168,000, and the interest rate is 6% fixed for 30 years. The lender also charges him 1 point of the loan which is which he paid out of his pocket. Points are prepaid interest. If Bill didn't pay the one point out of his pocket the lender would have tacked it on the contract agreed-upon interest rate of 6%, oh and the interest rate would have been adjusted to 7%, representing the one point not paid. Making his monthly mortgage payments $1,117.70 which would be an increase of $110.37 monthly. The property has two bedrooms in which each unit is being rented out for $750 per unit for a total of $1,500 in Gross rental income.

Note: This is not a Section8 situation.

Each tenant has eight months left on their lease. But the apartment rental market is commanding $850. Bill's reasoning is, once the eight months are up, he will raise the rent to its market value. Also, this is a separate utility situation. See chapter 4. The tenant pays the electricity, gas, heat yeah, and the owner pays the water, Insurance, property taxes, maintenance and repairs.

The properties annual operating data looks this way:

Gross Operating Income $18,000

Minus Additional Income $0

Gross Operating Expenses:

Utilities

Electric (Tenant)

Gas (Tenant)

Heat/Oil (Tenant)

Water $1800 (Owner)

Expenses:

Insurance $75 this is a monthly premium paid by Owner

Property Taxes $2,150 (Owner Pays)

Repairs and Maintenance $2,000 (Owner Pays)

Owner's Total Expenses $6,025

Annual Gross Operating Income $18,000

Minus Owner's Expenses $6,025

Equals $11,975 Net operating Income

But don't forget, throughout a 12-month period Bill has been making a monthly mortgage payment of $1007.83

$1007.83x12= $12087.96

Bill's annual debt service (aka monthly mortgage payment) total is $12,087.60

Now we have to subtract this figure from the NOI or Net operating Income figure of $11,975.

$12087.96	Total monthly mortgage payments for 12 months
-$11975.00	Property's net operating income
$112.96	The property is producing a negative cash flow.

Meaning that the property rental income is not enough to satisfy all of the annual debt that needs to be repaid. Alligator!!! In spite of this, Bill (emphasis added) is okay with coming out of his pocket for a while because again his position is once the tenant's 8 months lease is up, he will raise the rent to its market value of $850. And turn it from a negative cash flow situation to a positive cash flow. In the meantime, he will have to come out of his pocket and make up the $112.96 negative cash flow his investment philosophy created. In addition to that, he is relying on the 10% appreciation factor, which will make the property's value worth 230,000, based upon his speculation. This type of investment strategy can be extremely dangerous because it is based on future housing market principles remaining the same. If his speculation comes to pass, he will be able to borrow 80% of the property's equity through what is called a Home Equity Line Of Credit. This is discussed in Chapter 26 in more detail.

$231,000 x 80% = $184800 minus the $168000 loan he obtained to buy the property leaving him with a cash out equity of $16800. This is a little less once the closing cost is subtracted.

Three months after taking ownership of the house one of the tenants became a company downsize casualty. Meaning he or she was laid off, and now cannot afford to make the $750 rent payments. All of a sudden Bill now is faced with the inevitable loss of rent in one of his apartments. In addition to this, interest rates have been raised. Which means that it costs more now to borrow money from the bank to buy property. So now houses in the area are not being done as fast, if at all.

This also means that the 10% appreciation factor Bill was counting on, will not come to fruition. A lot of real estate investors work the appreciation angle. They will invest in the property just for the sake of the appreciation it offers, as long as the rent will carry the property. Then once it appreciates, they will use a Cash Out Equity refinancing technique to pay up the old loan, and replace it with a new loan, and use the additional cash taken out of the property to invest in other properties. This form of investing is extremely dangerous.

This is why I would never encourage you or anyone else to be an Appreciation Investor. The appreciation investment approach is fraught (filled with) ways you can be financially destroyed. Scenario analysis: where did Bill go wrong? First of all, Bill invested way too much capital into the property just to capitalize on a 10% appreciation rate. He assumed (like so many) that the rent was a guarantee, and he took for granted that the property would appreciate at 10% annually. Remember unlike the urban communities where real estate is typically moderate to very cheap in value, the wealthier areas the properties are located, the more susceptible these areas are subject to price manipulation. Some investors will invest in the area where the media and social housing experts say they should. They will say things like with interest rates being historically low now is a good time to invest in real estate or buy that home you always wanted. Not!

Scenario #2 using the Property Equity Niche Investment approach. Shirley finds a two-family house in the urban community where she has resided all of her life. She has been reading and studying the Property Equity Investment Approach that this book promotes and feels comfortable with the level of knowledge and understanding she has acquired. Now she's ready to make her first property purchase. She has been saving Her money for a while for some type of investment opportunity. Now the time has come for her money to go to work for her!

She finds a two-family house that has two bedrooms on each floor, and there is an attic with two additional rooms that can be combined with the second floor, to make it a four-bedroom apartment. Both departments will be rented out to section 8 approved applicants, and she knows that Section 8 pays $750 for two bedrooms and $1,500 for four bedrooms. Shirley has performed her due diligence. And has decided it's a go.

This is what her due diligence revealed. The property has a tax debt of $4,500 but she didn't have to worry about the pre-existing utility debt owed. Fortunately for her, she was able to locate the property owner of record, who wasn't interested in the property any longer, and was willing to sell his ownership interest in the property for $20,000. She counters with $16,250. He accepts her counteroffer. She asked for permission to enter the property, which was granted from the owner she assessed the damages, had an appraisal done, and had an inspection done. After her contractor assessed the internal and external physical condition of the property, it was determined by him that it would cost $1,000 to restore it. The appraisal report came back, and this is what it looked like:

- The "as restored" value of the property is $115000
- The "as is" value of the property is $6500 The Title Search showed that there were no additional liens on the property, and the Inspection Report showed no major damages due to insect infestation.

Shirley knew she would be receiving a total of $2,250 in Gross rental income for renting out both Apartments. The first-floor rent would be $750, and the second-floor rent would be $1,500. They're separate utilities. The tenant pays for gas and electricity. While the owner pays the water source and heat or oil. The total amount of Shirley out-of-pocket cost associated with the purchase of the property was $30,500. This amount includes restoration, property inspection, property insurance, inspection report, appraisal report and attorney fees. The real estate potential market value after the restoration process, based upon the appraisal report is $115,000.

Now if we subtract Shirley's total property purchase cost of $16,250 and the associated tax debt cost of $4,500, the total would be $20,750. Then we would subtract this total cost from the appraisal report 'as restored" value of $115,000. The difference between these two figures ($115,000 -$20,750 would be $94,250. This gives Shirley a return of 459%. $94,250 / $20,500 * 100% equals 459%. This is a very impressive rate of return on her investment dollars. Can you now see the power of buying inner-city physically distressed properties using the Property Equity Niche Investment approach?

Take a look now at the fine points of the system. Shirley bought the property with cash way below its as-is market value, and by doing so, she established a 459% property equity return on her money. Meaning that since she bought the property itself for only $16,250 and factoring in the tax debt of $4,500. Shirley capital investment is $20,750. In this case her money really went to work for her. This is the advantage of using the property Equity Niche investment approach. There's no debt on the property.

Whenever Shirley feels as though she is ready, she can

borrow against the property's equity of 115 thousand dollars and receive 80% of it which is $92,000. This will give her the financial ability to purchase more property using the same investment system. The borrowing on the property's equity allows her to take a substantial amount of tax-free money out of the property and have the government Section 8 guaranteed rent program pay the monthly mortgage payments. How awesome is that!

In this scenario Shirley had enough money saved up to make this work out, but don't forget, I have also provided you in this book a way to raise the capital needed to make this kind of deal happen. Poor Bill, if he had been educated on the Dynamics of the Property Equity Niche Investment Approach, he would have had the foresight to discern that the appreciation investment approach he was relying on represented a financial hazard.

So, as you can see by comparing scenario number one appreciation investing which resulted in Bill dealing with an Alligator, and scenario number 2 using the Property Equity Niche Investment Approach, which resulted in Shirley owning a Gold Mine. It makes sense to at least initially target urban community properties versus properties in the wealthy areas. Two different investment areas, controlled by two different dynamics ending with two contrasting results! Alligator or Gold Mine? You decide.

Author's Thoughts: we live in a society where critical and analytical thought seems to be in short supply. As a result of this undeniable fact, some are easily manipulated to respond in a certain way, based upon the so-called expert advice they receive. You don't want to be Bill in the scenario of one who adopted a real estate investment strategy called appreciation investing, just because he was informed that is the best way to invest in real estate, my words to you are learn, understand, and then engage (invest)!

21 Handyman's Special

The Property Equity Niche Investment delight. What is a handyman special? A handyman special is a house that typically requires extensive repairs and restorations, and because of its current condition, it is sold at a steep discount, in comparison to its restored value. You will generally find these types of properties being advertised in the newspapers classified section. Typically, in these situations the property is in need of extensive work including but not limited to:

Plumbing

Electrical

Carpentry

Roofing

Also expect to do some painting as well. It could also possibly be lead contaminated, and in which case you must proceed with caution. The property inspection should detect this. The owner will generally (but there are exceptions) have no debt on the property such as taxes, utilities or any other type. The property will usually have insurance on it to protect the owner from fire, vandalism etc. More often than not, not the current owner purchased the property from some other source, (i.e. private owner, or city) to make a quick profit on the resale of the property. Usually, they are more seasoned concerning the real estate grind. So, they have a good eye, and understanding for property valuation, as it relates to these kinds of properties. And what they purchase the property for, versus what they sell it for, is based on what they determine the property value to be. These types of investors are also proficient (highly skilled) at calculating their acceptable rate of return on their investment dollars. They do this by first determining the value of the property.

By now in this book, you should know the difference between your cash equity in the property which is based on the As is value, and the equity return that the As Restored value yields. Haven't stated this, here's scenario number one Derrick is interested in purchasing a three-family house with two bedrooms on each floor that was advertised in the newspaper as a Handyman Special. The asking price is $30,000 cash. So, Derrick scheduled a walkthrough with the current owner and went to look at the property accompanied by his contractor.

The contractor assessed the condition of the property and determined that the property was in need of significant plumbing, electrical and carpentry work. The roof was in good condition, but a complete paint job was needed inside and out of the property. Overall, it was structurally sound! His contractor gave him an itemized estimation cost to fully rehabilitate the property of $15,000.) Labor costs would be $8,000 and materials and supplies would be approximately $7,000.

And at this point Derrick contacts his realtor and asks her how much the last 3 family units in the area he's looking at sold for. His realtor checks the computer and gives him a sales comparison analysis of $125,000. He thanks her and then hangs up the phone. Derrick, being a seasoned real estate investor, recognizes that he has a potential Goldmine opportunity. So, what he does is pulls out his checkbook, and writes the check for $5,000 as a down payment on the property. What he did once he realized that the Sales Comparison Analysis was appealing to him was moved to secure the property, so no one could come after him and steal the deal away from him.

He takes out his purchase sales agreement contract that he keeps with him for such occasions. Once the current owner takes the check written for $5,000 as a down payment and signs the contract Derrick at this point controls the fate (or final outcome) of this real estate investment deal. Remember this important move, in your real estate grind dealings. Derrick made sure that the contract had the Subject To clause in it.

Note. Once again, the "subject to" clause in this contract sets the condition of the contract by the buyer, (in this case Derrick) , that has to be met in order for the sale to go through.

Derrick's sales purchase agreement "subject to" clause stated the following:

- a satisfactory title search
- a satisfactory inspection report
- a satisfactory appraisal report

The closing date on the house was made 15 business days from the day of the contract signing. This gave Derrick ample time to obtain all of the information he needed. He then began his due diligence. The title search, inspection report and appraisal report are all ordered. In this scenario, since he is going to flip the property, he will use these documents to provide the next potential buyer with.

All the requested reports came back satisfactory, it is now time to close on the property and take full ownership! The appraisal report showed that the property "as is" value is

$65,000. and the “as restored value is $122,500. The current asking price was $30,000. Now let’s look at what the numbers consist of as it relates directly to the property itself.

- as restored market value $122,500
- as is market value $65,000
- Cash purchase price $30,000

Derrick is one of those investors who seek a 60% return on his invested dollars, and this deal is no different. So Derrick places an ad in the newspaper classified section for one week stating Handyman’s Special. Asking $50,000 cash, approximately 66% return on his cash investment.

Note. This is a gross figure that does not take into account what the tax liability payment in this deal would be. Your tax expert will inform you of what you would owe in taxes for deals like this.

This word Firm is incorporated into the Ad to convey to the prospective interested investor that the asking price is nonnegotiable! As I am sure you have discovered by now with the Property Equity Niche Investment Approach, I like to use the terms like As Restored market value, As is market value and cash purchase price. Obviously, the cash purchase price represents the out-of-pocket dollars used to purchase the real estate, in this scenario it is $30,000.

Then there is the property's “As is” market value. In this scenario it is $65,000. As well as the “As Restored” market value, in this scenario it is $122,500. Now let’s dissect this scenario from a microscopic perspective. Derrick invested $30,000 cash into the property. The property’s “As is” value was

$65,000 and the "As Restored" value was $122,500. The difference between the purchase price and the "As is" value is $35,000. $65,000-$30000 = $35000. Since Derrick expects a 60% return on his investment, he will have to determine what is 60% of the property purchase price of $30,000.

$30,000 x 60% = $18,000. Add the $18,000 to $30,000 and you get $48,000. This figure represents a 60% return on the property purchase price of $30,000. Since typically you wouldn't sell a property for $48,000, Derrick decides to set the resale price to $50,000.

So, in essence, in order for Derrick to receive a gross profit of at least 60% on his capital investment of $30,000 he is going to sell the property for $50,000 cash.

I presented this scenario to you so that you could see and understand how the Handyman's Special buying and selling process can be worked. Please pay close attention to what I am about to state. "By no means am I suggesting that you buy for a quick resale, but just in case you decide to buy a Handyman's Special for resale this strategy is available to you.

Caution. In the event that you do decide to buy and resale the property, make sure you discuss it with your lawyer and accountant first! Right now, though, for you as a beginner, your focus needs to be on establishing a constant monthly or weekly flow of income. Which comes by renting out your apartments to Section8 tenants. Having explored this course of real estate investment, we are now going to look at the same purchasing opportunity using a different approach.

This time the Handyman's Special is going to be qualified

for a buy hold and rent out purpose. Scenario #2 features Derrick is interested in buying a Three house that was advertised in the newspaper as a Handyman's Special. The asking price is $30,000 cash. The property has 2 bedrooms in each unit. Derrick decided that the property is worth a look, so he and his contractors made arrangements to see the property. After his contractor assesses the condition of the property no, he determines that it is in need of significant plumbing, electrical and carpentry work. The roof is good. It will need a new paint job, inside and out, but structurally it is sound!

The estimated cost to have the necessary rehabilitation and pant job needed will cost Derrick $15,000. The contractor's breakdown is labor cost $8000 and materials and supplies $7000. (See Chapter 3 only dealing with your contractor.) At this point Derrick calls his realtor and asked how much the last Three family property in the area he did is interested in sell for. call. His realtor checks the computer and gives him a Sales Comparison Analysis of $125,000. So, he thanks her and then hangs up the phone. Derrick being a seasoned real estate investor recognized that he has a potential Goldmine opportunity. So, what he does is pull out his checkbook and write a check for $5,000 as a down payment on the property.

What he did once he realized that the Sales Comparison Analysis his realtor gave him was appealing. He moved to secure the property so no one could come after him and steal the deal away from him. So, he takes out his purchase sales agreement contract that he keeps with him. Once the current owner takes the check written for $5,000 as a down payment and signs the contract, Derrick now controls the fate of the property. So, remember this important move in your real estate grind dealings.

Always move to lock the property once you decide it's a potential go.

Derrick made sure that the contract had the Subject To clause in it. It stated this purchase sale agreement is subject to:

- A satisfactory title insurance report, performed by an insurance company.
- A satisfactory inspection report
- An Acceptable appraisal report

The closing date on the house was made 15 business days from the day of the contract signing. Derrick now begins his due diligence. He requested that a property inspector do an inspection on the property. Also requested that an appraisal be done. All the requested reports came back satisfactory. It is now time to close on the property and take full ownership! The appraisal report revealed that the property "As is" value is $65,000 and the "As Restored" market value is $122,500.

The current owner was only asking for $30,000 cash. Section 8 is paying $750 for two bedrooms. That means his gross monthly income will be $2,150. There is no mortgage, and he will retain most of the rental income produced by the property. (With the exception of the Operating Expenses) His situation looks as follows:

- The "As Restored" market value of the property is $122,500.
- The "As is" market value of the property is $65,000.
- The "purchase price" is $30,000 cash.
- Restoration costs $15,000.
- Note. Cost overrun is possible, so make allowance for that

in your restoration costs budget. A 20% allowance is the norm.

- The other cost, such as attorney fees, inspection report, and appraisal report total is $2,500.

Once the property is repaired, its equity return value will be $75,000. Add this number to Derrick's capital investment in the property of $47,500, for a total As Restored market value of $122,500. Once the restoration is done. Once Derrick has reached the point in his investing where he is comfortable with the Home Equity Line of Credit, he will be in a position to pull his capital investment of 47,500 out of the property, (tax free) to purchase other properties.

Here's how it can be done. A lender typically will lend 80% of an income producing property's equity. In this scenario, the property is $122,500 and Derrick can borrow 80% of that, providing he can meet the lender's lending requirements. $122,500 x 80= $98,000. That means Derrick will receive $98,000 of the property's equity. Derrick recaptured his capital investment of $47,500, plus an additional $50,500 for a total of $98,000 (minus closing cost). Don't forget that the housing authority is largely subsidizing his loans' monthly payments, by sending him a check every month, in the form of rental income for doing them a favor by renting out his apartments to their Section8 approved recipients.

Author thoughts: I know by now you have to be impressed by the real estate grind, as well as the Property Equity Niche Investment Approach. The options you have been presented with in this chapter was to help you see that Handyman's Special type of properties can be very profitable to you as well. Once you develop an understanding of property prequalification and valuation, it will be easy for you to identify a Goldmine opportunity, where others can only see an eyesore. A lot of urban communities in the United States are saturated with opportunities like we covered in this chapter. Also remember to always know the reasoning behind you going after a particular piece of property. Don't just buy property just for the sake of buying it. Look to see how you are going to maximize the property's income potential.

Dating back to ancient times, economic prosperity has always been available to the self-motivators. Nothing has changed since then, except the mindset of some. One's motivation regarding mental and physical engagement oftentimes is predicated on where their level of interest lies, and if they are not passionately interested in something, they will be less inclined to get involved with it. So, in light of this proven fact, it is my hope that this book sparks a meaningful level of interest in you, that will subsequently bear the fruit of personal economic prosperity for you and yours!

22 My Bond Street Lesson

"My Experience can be your best teacher"

Sometimes in life it is not really about what you find yourself going through, as much as what it is that you should learn from what you are going through. I remember my first experience in the world of real estate investing was by way of a property foreclosure auction. I was driving down Bond Street, a street in New Haven, enroute to a particular destination, when a property on the right side of the street caught my eye. It was a two-family unit with a public auction sign on it. The sign had the auction date, time and the cashier's check amount of $4,500 in order to bid on the property.

At that moment, I decided I wanted to purchase my first company owned real estate property. At this time, I was the President of a real estate investment company my cousin and I formed. Since it was started with very limited funds, I didn't have too many cash purchase options. Since I felt I had a good understanding of the real estate investment grind, I was perfectly comfortable with proceeding in the matter. The next thing I did was go to my attorney's office to find out how I could go about gauging the extent of the property's interior damage.

After I informed him of the details of the public auction that I knew of, and then expressed my desire to see what the inside looked like, he responded by saying "the state law prohibits you from entering the property until the day of the auction." He then made a call and let me know that it was a bank foreclosure. which I figured as such. Evidently whomever the borrower/s where they got behind in their monthly mortgage payments, and now the bank was foreclosing on the property.

I took in everything he said and then said, “Okay.” I let him know that I appreciated the information, and then I left his office. While I was in my car driving. I kept replaying in my mind two things, how appealing the property was to me, and what my attorney said about it being unlawful to enter the property before the public auction date. Against my attorney’s professional advice, I made a reckless decision to find out what the inside of the property looked like. Please note.

Caution. I do not suggest that you take this course of action because it is illegal. I was trespassing on private property. This was against the law!

I went back around the neighborhood and found four willing individuals to go inside of the property. Once at the property, we all went towards the backyard, because there was a window boarded up, that was going to be our means of entry. After the board was removed, I instructed everyone to check the property out from the basement up to the attic area. I gave them a flashlight and wished them well, while I waited for them to return. Lol. One of them came back and informed me that it was in good condition. I entered to do an inspection of my own, especially now that I knew no wildlife, or any form of life had taken residence inside! Lol.

I started in the basement, and worked my way up to the attic, no and at each level I became more and more impressed, but the attic was the kicker. Apparently, the previous owners converted the attic into an efficiency. It contained two bedrooms, a full bathroom, a kitchen stove and a refrigerator. It was at that point when I broke the real estate investor’s code. I fell in love with the property. I began to envision all the rent money I was going to receive by renting to Section8 tenants. In my mind, a good opportunity had just become great! It was a go! I would bid on the property at the public auction.

I became so blind by the interior condition of the property and the income producing potential it possessed, that I neglected to do any due diligence. Major mistake! Due diligence in this situation would be to qualify the property by going downtown to City Hall's registry of deeds department, to find out how much mortgage debt was on the property.

In cases like a bank foreclosure auction, there is not going to be any other debt on the property, because the bank is going to pay any debt, outside of its own, in full (i.e. city taxes) Why? Because if the bank doesn't at least pay in full any city or federal tax debt, and either one of these entities forecloses on the property, the bank's mortgage debt will be completely wiped out by this foreclosure auction. Your due diligence in this situation would also be to determine what the approximate value of the property is based upon a sale's comparable analysis, which as you know is free and can be obtained through your realtor.

If I had requested one in this situation, I would have learned that the property's value once the restoration work was done on it, would be around $110,000 to $115000. Since you are not allowed to enter the property until the day of the auction, you will not be able to perform your additional due diligence such as property inspection or appraisal report. An informal valuation report, (Sales Comparable Analysis), will have to do. This is why the more sophisticated real estate investors purchase bank foreclosures. My only focus from that point on was to make sure that I had the cashier's check for $4,500 to bid on the property, and failure was not an option. As far as me not securing the winning bid.

<u>The day of the Auction</u>. It was raining off and on all morning. There was a large crowd despite the weather condition. Those who would be bidding on the property were inside already with their flashlights trying to inspect as much of the property as possible before the bidding began. Inside the property, a lot of bidders were talking on their cellphones. I overheard one guy say, “It looks like a go!” Once back outside the auctioneer had all the bidders on the property step to the front with the cashier’s check for $4,500. Once to the front he explained that he would open the bid at a certain amount, and that each bid solicited from that point on would be $5,000 increments (increases). He started off at 45,000, and once someone repeated the dollar amount the bid went up to $45,500 and so on until someone secured the property.

By the time it reached $55,000, most of the bidders had already left, and at this stage in the auction there were only three bidders, two others and myself. The auctioneer asked for a bid of $55,000 of which my bidding opponent yelled $55,000. I then yelled out $60,000. The auctioneer then repeated my bid for $65,000 to which someone answered $65,500. So, I countered with seventy thousand. The auctioneer then repeated my bid and asked for a bid of $70,000. No one spoke to which the auctioneer said, “Seventy thousand. Going once. Going twice. Sold to the bidder of $70,000.

I secured the auction bid on the property, but at what cost? For me, now it was time to do the work on the property, so that I could rent it out to Section8 approved applicants, and at some point, in time borrow against the equity in the property.

Now remember, I secured the auction purchase bid on the property for $70,000 but I only brought a Cashier's Check in the amount of $4,500 to the public auction.

So where was the remaking balance of $65,500 coming from? It was coming from the financing I arranged before the auction.

I had 30 days from the day of the auction to satisfy the balance (65,000), or risk losing the four thousand and five hundred dollars and the right to take ownership of the property.

I share this experience of mine with you not because I'm leading you down the path of buying bank foreclosure property, but I do this for two reasons. 1. To show you that the Property Equity Niche Investment Approach can be applied when buying bank foreclosures and 2. to show you, that if you do decide to pursue this investment route, through a public auction in the inner city, what to expect, as well as what to safeguard yourself from.

Actually, this experience is what motivated me to create the Property Equity Niche Investment Approach. If this investment system was already formed during that time, I would have approached this situation from a totally different angle.

Now let me list where I went wrong.

1. I fell in love with the property.
2. I didn't perform my due diligence.
3. I should have obtained a Sales Comparison Analysis and then compared it to the Depreciated Value Accumulation

Approach (covered in chapter 8).
4. I never determined what the property as is or the As Restored value was.
5. I didn't check the legitimacy of the Efficiency set up in the attic, because had I done so, I would have found out that in order for a property to have an Efficiency arrangement, there are specific state and housing laws that must be complied with. I made the assumption that just because the attic was already converted into one, it was legal.

This factor is key when using the P.E.N.I.A (i.e., The Property Equity Niche Investment Approach) system. The property housing zone classification was only for a Two Family. Shortly after the auction, I was contacted by a housing official, and informed me that the previous owner was operating the property as an illegal Three Family unit. Which is in violation of the state's housing and building codes. He then formally requested that I remove the bathroom and kitchen set up, of which I agreed to. And if that wasn't enough, I received word from the mortgage broker handling the deal that the lender was aware of the illegal set up, and that in order for the loan to go through, I would have to make sure that the property is changed back into its legally zoned Two-Family status.

The credit line that I had with Lowe's was not enough to cover costs of the materials and supplies. So, I was running around town trying to borrow money from certain family members until the property was up and running. I even fell behind on payments to my contractor. The property that I thought was a Star, was starting to look more like a Scar! I engaged in a bidding war for the property and ultimately paid too much for it.

Here's another way I could have approached this situation.

I should have raised additional private capital for a cash purchase beforehand. Instead of seeking financing from a lender. Once I determined the property's worth based on the Depreciated Value Accumulation, I should have then established the amount I would be willing to pay for the property and be committed to walk away if the auction bid exceeded that amount.

This is why I'm not recommending this course of action (purchasing foreclosures) for those of you just starting out, in the real estate grind field. Whereas, if you buy a Handyman's Special, or other physically distressed property in the Urban Community, you can put the necessary protection on yourself by including the Subject To clause in the purchase sales agreement contract. In retrospect (as I look back), I now realize that those investors at the auction, who walked away at $55,000 were standing firm on their investment principle. This is why, it is said in the real estate investment field that "You make your money when you purchase the property."

Why, because the less you pay of the As Restored property value (in its run-down condition), the higher your equity position will be once the restoration process is complete. As illustrated in Chapter 9. Property foreclosure purchases are best executed by Cash Buyers that have a firm understanding of the property prequalification and valuation process.

Author's Thoughts: In life, one never knows where their interest truly lies, or their level of commitment to it until they encounter an experience that challenges it. Because then and only then will it be known to that person, if they were ever fully committed, or whether or not it was just a whim (a sudden fancy).

Not initially prospering in something you set out to do does not mean that it's not for you. It just may not be time to flourish in it!

Unshakable vision is like an anchor that keeps you resolute in your quest, don't allow your current circumstances to hinder you from remaining process driven, getting what you need during that time, to achieve what it is that you set out to accomplish! If you find yourself identifying with these words, you have already embarked on the journey of believing in yourself. Don't look to anyone to validate you, or your God given potential. Focus on acquiring and developing the skills you need to succeed in your field of choice. And during this process, watch the company you keep!

23 Buying Real Estate Already Rented Out

Up until this point in the book we have looked at different real estate investment scenarios that were solely based on the purchasing rundown, vacant properties. But in this chapter, we're going to cover buying real estate in the inner cities that are rented out to Section 8 tenants, for those of you that may be presented with the opportunity to buy such properties. OK let's begin. Mary is looking in the local newspaper classified section on real estate, and she notices an ad taking out that says, “For Sale by owner”. It’s a two-family unit, with 2 bedrooms in each apartment. Asking price $115,000. The address is 215 Bullway Ave. Great rental income. Call Paul at 475-345-4895, from Monday through Friday anytime between 5 PM to 9:00 PM.

Mary, being a student of The Property Equity Niche Investment Approach, feels confident that the knowledge and understanding she has obtained through the studying of this system qualifies her to now buy her first property. So, she calls the phone number listed, speaks with Paul and schedules an appointment to see the property. Mary knows that in order to make a purchase offer on the property, she has to 1st prequalify the property and then value it. So, the first thing she does is go to the county’s recorder department/registrars of deeds department to retrieve the information needed to thoroughly prequalify the property. She discovers that the property was built 20 years ago, and its original value was $115,000. There are no visible recorded liens on the property, or a bank mortgage note. Meaning that the current owner never borrowed any money from the bank against the equity in the property.

Mary writes down this important information and leaves. While back at home, she values the property using the depreciated accumulation method covered in chapter eight. Original property value $115,000 / 27.5 years, IRS depreciation. Equals $4,181.82. This figure is for one year only. Now she takes the $4, 181.82 and multiplies it by seven years which gives her $29,272.73. But wait there are seven and a half years of value depreciation left. Mesha must take the figure $4,181 .82 divided by two to represent the half year.

$4,181.82 / 2 = 2,090.91

$29,272.73 + 2,090.91 + $31,363.64 hey sure

So based upon the depreciation value accumulation this income producing property is worth $31,363.64. And because this is an income producing property it's highly unlikely that its owner will sell it to Mary for $31,363.64. So, she will rely on the net operating income combined with the cap rate approach. Using the Annual Property Operating Data Form. This valuation method is worksheet #3 1. Before we proceed, I want to take the time out to acquaint you with this valuation approach. Also know that the effectiveness of this valuation approach is contingent on your ability to establish the capitalization rate (cap rate) for the type of property you're interested in purchasing. This can be accomplished by the property owners providing you with the relevant information to fill out an Annual Property Operating Data Form.

But first what is a capitalization rate (Cap Rate)? Simply put the capitalization rate is the rate of return as a percentage for investors on their capital investment based on the income the property produces. It is also used as a valuation tool to determine the respective property's value, based upon the net operating income it produces. This is done by dividing the property's net operating income (NOI) by the cap rate of a specific investment property. (e.g., NOI / cap rate = value of property.

Note. Typically, inner city properties have high cap rates, in the double-digit area, which also means on the flip side that their values will invariably be low. Review Chapter 8 on how this value principle works. Now let's look at what an Annual Property Operating Data Form looks like. From a practical standpoint, the property's cap rate is not included in this layout because this valuation method combines the Net Operating Income and the cap rate, so it would be wise to include it at the top as shown below.

Property's Cap Rate _________%

A POD/Annual Property Operating Data:

Gross Schedule Income (GSI)

$________________________________

Other income $_________________________ other income would be if the property had coin operated washers and dryers, a rental art garage etc.

Vacancy allowance/credit $________________________ (by renting out the Section 8 vacancy should not be an issue.)

= Gross Operating Income

$____________________________________

Annual Operating Expenses:

Utilities:

Electric $___________________________

Gas $______________________________

Water/Sewer $______________________

Heat/Oil$___________________________

Insurance $________________________

Property Taxes $____________________

Maintenance $______________________

Repairs $___________________________

Total Operating Expenses $______________________

Gross Operating Income $______________________ Minus (-) $_________________________ total annual operating expenses = $_______________________________ net operating income (NOI).

Now divide the NOI by the cap rate (e.g. NOI$__________/ Cap rate $____________ % equal $_______value of property.

Questions #5

Are there Section 8 tenants? Hopefully they are, but if they are not, you can always wait until their lease is up, and then decide what you want to do. In this type of situation, I suggest that an exception to the rule can be made. If they are a good tenant, then having them relocate would not be prudent (wise of you) or fair to the tenant.

#6

Are you in possession of any security deposits? The issue of security deposits was discussed in Chapter 7 knowing what the landlord tenant relationship laws state. Your real estate attorney will be able to inform you of what the state laws say about this particular issue.

#7

How much are the property taxes? Obviously paying the property taxes is of importance to any landlord, because failure to do so will result in the county placing a tax lien on the property first, and if you continue to disregard the notices they send you , they will either conduct a tax lien certificate , a tax deed sale or foreclose on the property directly through court proceedings , on the grounds of tax delinquency (nonpayment of taxes).

#8

What utilities do the landlord pay? You ask this question to get a feel of what your utility bill as a landlord may be.

#9

May I see your IRS 1040 form schedule E? This is a tax form that investment property owners fill out listing what the income and expenses were for the property. You request this form because the tendency for the numbers to be accurate are more likely, especially since if the numbers are fraudulent, the owner could possibly face a fine or federal imprisonment for lying on his or her tax form. So you request this form because the chances of the numbers being played down is less likely than if they gave you the same numbers by word of mouth.

Mary reviews the list of questions for the following day and finds it satisfactory. The following day: Mary arrives on time, and Paul is waiting for her. The two greet each other and Mary begins to take notice of the outside condition of the property and is impressed by what she sees. At least on the surface. Paul beforehand has gotten the approval of both tenants to show the interior of the apartments to Mary. Mary in preparation of her appointment jotted down a few questions the night before. The following day listed below are the questions she asked Paul.

Why are you selling the property?

How long has it been on the market?

How long is each tenant lease?

How much is each apartment being rented for?

Are they Section 8 tenants?

Are you in possession of any security deposits?

How much are the property taxes?

What utilities does the landlord pay?

May I see your IRS1040 form schedule E?

These questions above help you also determine what your purchase offer is going to be. Now let's go over each question so that you can understand why asking these questions is so important to your purchase offer.

Question 1: why are you selling the property? You asked this question to get a better feel of how anxious and committed they are to sell call Qwaia what is five the property.

Question 2: How long has the property been on the market? The reasoning behind this question is if they just recently put the property on the market, they may not be too inclined to accept a purchase offer that discounts the asking price by much. But if the property has been on the market for 120 days or more, they will be more inclined to accept a purchase offer that represents a reduction of the asking price. This type of situation represents a great investment opportunity for you.

Question 3: how long is each tenant's lease? For whatever reason the property owner may not be charging the tenant market rents. If that is the case, you want to know so that you can once their lease is up rent out to Section 8 tenants.

Question 4: how much is each apartment being rented out for? The reason you asked this question is so that you will know if the apartments are being rented out at Section 8 rates. You will not know what Section 8 is paying based on the number of bedrooms, because you are going to check with the housing authority.

Mary is also satisfied with the way the tenants have maintained the inside of the apartments. After she completed her walkthrough of the entire property, she and Paul go outside to discuss the questions of interest that need to be addressed. She starts off with the first question on the list.

Question 1: Why are you selling the property? I am just too old, and am tired of being a landlord, so I just wanted to get rid of the property, says Paul.

Question 2: How long has it been on the market? For four months now.

Question 3: How long is each tenant lease? The first-floor tenant is about one year into a two-year lease, and the 2nd floor tenant is approximately six months into a two-year lease.

Question 4: How much is each apartment being rented out for? The first floor and 2nd floor are being rented out at $750 each.

Question 5: are they both Section 8 tenants? Yes

Question 6: Are you in possession of any security deposits? Yes. First and last month's seven rent Paul replies.

Question 7: How much are the property taxes? $1,200 Paul states.

Question 8: which utilities does the landlord pay? I pay the water sewer and heat oil bill. The electricity and gas are paid by the tenant.

Mary responds with, “how much is the annual heating bill?” Paul says, “it ranges anywhere from $2,800 to $3,300.” Mary replies, “it could be worse I guess.” Mary then requests to see Paul IRS form 1040 schedule. Paul then becomes quiet, so Mary informs him that she is only interested in verifying the annual expenses, as it relates to the property, not his personal income and expenses. This is why she's only requesting to see that particular form. Paul then says OK fine. I will provide you with that information tomorrow. Mary seems concerned by such a delayed reaction, especially since tomorrow will be the day she presents her purchase offer. So, Paul attempts to lessen her fears by saying I'm confident that the numbers I gave you are pretty accurate, therefore all you will need to do tomorrow is cross reference the numbers I gave you, with the numbers on the IRS form 1040 schedule. She looks relieved and stares you're right!

Investor's Notes. When buying property that's already rented out, do not make it a practice of crunching your numbers without the IRS 1040 Schedule E document. After writing in her pad all of the information gathered, she thanks Paul, and says "I look forward to tomorrow, me too Paul responds.

They shake hands and Mary gets into her car and drives off. Mary now has most of the information needed to crunch the numbers on the property. O but wait, another expense she will have as the landlord is insurance, and her insurance policy may be more or less than Paul.

Following the suggestion stated in Chapter 3, she contacts her insurance agent Dexter. She gives him the type of property (investment property, she is thinking about buying, its physical characteristics, and its location. He informs her that based on the information she has given him, her monthly premium payments will be $125.00. Now Mary is ready to crunch the numbers.

For this Mary relies on the Annual Property Operating Data. Also known as the APOD.

Here's what everything looks like:

Gross Schedule Income: $18,000

Other Income: 0 (other income would be if there was a coin operated washer and dryers in the basement)

Minus

Vacancy Allowance: $0 (by renting out to Section8, you should not have a real vacancy issue)

Gross Operating Income: $18,000

Operating Expenses:

<u>Utilities</u>

Electric: $0. (Tenant pays)

Gas:0. (tenant pays)

Water/Sewer $ 300.00 (landlord pays)

Insurance Policy (for 1year) $ 1,500 (landlord Pays)

Property Taxes $ 1,200 (landlord Pays)

Heat/Oil $ 3,300 (landlord pays)

Total Operating Expenses $ 6,300 (This figure represents Mary's operating expenses for 1 year).

Gross Operating Income $18,000 -

Total Operating Expenses $ 6,300

= $11, 700.00 This figure represents the Net Operating Income (discussed in chapter 11).

The Capitalization Rate (cap rate) on this property is 13.

How you would determine the value of this property using the Valuation Method, is by dividing the N.O.I of ($ 11,700) by .13 (the cap rate), which equals $ 90,000.

Mary has established the property to be worth (based on these numbers) $ 90,000. Because she is practicing The Property Equity Niche Investment Approach, she is going to present a Cash offer of 55,000. This represents about 60% of the value she determined the property to be worth.

Now she is expecting Paul to reject this offer, and counter it with an offer. If he does, she will counter with an offer. So, she meets with Paul the next day at 11, he presents her with the requested form. She verifies the numbers, and then presents an offer of 55,000 cash, as he anticipated Paul counters with a price of 65,000 Mary looks at it and says I am firm on my offer. Paul looks at her, smiles and says good. They shook hands, then they both signed the purchase and sales agreement that Mary brought with her. She writes in the agreed-upon purchase price, and the terms of the deal, along with the Subject To provisions.

Once the contract is signed by both the seller and the buyer, the contract is to be given to Mary's attorney with a copy given to the seller. Mary then takes out her checkbook and writes out a check for Five Thousand Dollars as a down payment. With the remaining balance to be paid once the Subject To clause has been satisfied! The closing date on the contract reads that it will take place 15 business days from the current date, at the buyer's attorney office. All ordered reports came back satisfactory and 15 days later, the closing took place as scheduled at Mary's attorney office. After all, agreed upon closing costs were paid by each party, Mary and Paul shake hands and wish each other well!

Mary is now officially a property owner.

This type of property buying scenario was incorporated into this book just to show you that The Property Equity Niche Approach can be executed even for property that's already rented out. Some sellers will call this strategy "low balling." But remember what type of investor you are (A Property Equity Niche Investor), and in order for you to buy Any property, it has to make economic sense to you!

The P.E.N.I.A investment strategy is a mindset, a strict discipline that requires a certain level of commitment and understanding. You buy property below market value, so just in case the housing market in the area you're invested in takes a sudden hit, if the property values begin to drop, your cash investment is still protected. Make sense?

Author's Thoughts: Your mind has the capacity to be the most powerful tool you have but just like any upcoming tradesmen/ investor, you must be taught how to use it effectively. I have embarked upon this literary journey, with a personal interest, devoted to ensuring you receive a basic quality, as well as a motivational product that will enable you to give Birth to the entrepreneurial seed in you. And all it requires is a commitment on your part to the learning process, and a willingness to believe that economic prosperity is your Birthright!!

24 Accessing the Equity In The Property

Accessing the free Gold (money) in your mine by implementing this last step in The Property Equity Niche Investment Approach. Congratulations! You are now at the defining moment in the book that epitomizes (that best represents) what this entire system is all about. How do you go about Accessing the Equity in Your Property? By taking out a Home Equity Line of Credit. Also known as a HELOC.

What is a Home Equity Line Of Credit/ HELOC. It is a loan in which a lender agrees to lend a maximum amount, within an agreed upon period, where the collateral is the borrower(s) Equity in his/ her property. Definition taken from Wikipedia

But the question you may have now is Why a Home Equity Line Of Credit? The following is a list of reasons why this form of financing is the more appealing way to go.

1.Lower Interest Rates

2. Lower Closing Costs

3. Lower Annual Percentage Rate (APR). Meaning the total costs of the loan is cheaper.

4. It Can be used like a credit card; in that you only pay interest on the portion of the principal loan amount you use.

5. It can be established as a revolving credit line. This means that the principal and interest payments you make, towards the amount of the credit line you use, is added back into the original loan amount.

The initial five steps of investment approach (i.e The prequalifying, valuation, purchasing, restoration, and renting out to Section 8 approved tenants) serves as the road map, that is designed to ultimately lead you to this most critical point. Because now it's time for you to access the monetary value that your Goldmine (property) possesses.

The buy Low and Sell high does not compare to the Buy at or Below the As is value of the property, rent out to section 8 approved tenants, and then, when you're ready, Cash Out on the property's equity approach. So now the question becomes, what are the advantages of holding the property and borrowing against the equity in it. When you borrow against the equity in your property, it is not classified as taxable income by the Internal Revenue Service. Once again, please contact your tax expert on this matter.

Just think about it this way. You get tithe opportunity to withdraw a large amount of Gold (your property's equity) from your investment property and have the Housing Authority Section 8 program dollars make the monthly payments for you, through the rent money you receive for renting out to those that have been approved to receive this government housing subsidy.

Note. A lender typically loans 80 % of a property's equity value (but this percentage could vary). This is called the loan to value ratio, or LTV.

For example, if you own a property that is worth $150,000, and there is no mortgage on the property. Based on the standard lending practice of a 80% loan to value ratio, the lender would be willing to lend you $120,000. Then there's the closing costs you must pay. Which normally is 3-5 percent of the overall loan. So, in this case it would be $ 120,000 X .03 = $ 3,600, or $ 120,000 X .05 = $6,000. This would leave you with still $ 30,000 of equity in your property.

This method of operating once fully understood, and properly executed, will enrich your social and economic position in more ways than you can ever imagine. The whole objective of this book is to show you how to make money in real estate, through a particular investment approach.

Now, I understand that people's learning curve will vary, and so everyone that reads and studies The Property Equity Niche Investment Approach, will not immediately grasp it all , and this is why I created The Real Estate Grind Consultation Company. I can be reached at **regpropertysolutions@gmail.com**. Any consultation needed; I will provide. Contact me so that we can discuss the various levels of consultation packages available to you.

It is my desire to have everyone that purchases this book, to be on one accord, so that collectively, there will be an Inner City distress property investment movement in America, that will positively impact the social, geographical and economic make up of these cities, and its inhabitants! And while I'm on this Accessing the Equity In Your Property issue, I might as well Sow a seed of economic prosperity over your life. So, position yourselves to receive the increase that will surely come your way. Once you do become financially strong, educate yourself some more in other investment areas, and really put your money to work for you.

Author's Thoughts: Throughout this book, I have not only shown you what your starting point should be once you become actively engaged in the real estate grind business, but I have also revealed to you in this chapter, what your end position should be as well, which is Mining the Gold from your Goldmine!!

25 Author Closing Thoughts

The author's thoughts throughout the book is my way of connecting with you mentally, emotionally, and spiritually. And by doing so, you would know that I am not some insulated (isolated) individual who's not qualified to speak on, or truly identify with your plight, and thus, disqualify myself from providing you with a viable (workable) solution to overcoming your problem. This is why I humbly submitted myself to you, as one that is very much a part of you, and a participant of the same struggles as you. And even more so, as one that allowed himself to fall victim to the inner presence of frustration, that emanated from being socially, educationally, and financially handicapped, in a society that offers so much opportunity to those willing to totally commit to being an achiever!

As much as it's hard to accept but a lot of times in life, our restrictive, poverty-stricken life is a direct result of our unwillingness to strive for better. And it's this type of attitude which breeds socioeconomic complacency! And where you find such an attitude, you will typically also find what I call a Compromised sense of contentment. By that I mean, you will oftentimes hear people that are destitute say "money isn't everything". Well, my belief is, the reason why they say that is because, it serves as a coping mechanism, to offset the real discontentment of a less than desirable life.

Now don't get me wrong. I am not saying that Money is everything. But I do think that a reasonable consensus would reveal that, having money does grant one more liberty, provides more security and comfort, as well as an intense need to guard it at all costs, for the sake of those loved ones that you are making a better way for. By contrast though, in these tough current economic times, there seems to be a socioeconomic awakening (by some actions) throughout America that conveys the message that, enough is enough! Those that have been accepting of marginalization, and disenfranchisement, are now taking proactive measures towards educational, social, and economic empowerment!

In this book I have endeavored to inform, challenge and motivate my readers to partake in the opportunities that the real estate industry offers. My studies and research over the years, with respect to the educated and financially literate in America uncovered an ostensible, undeniable fact. And that is, the vast majority of wealthy Americans, as well as the wealthy abroad, all own real estate.

This book was composed as an Introductory Beginners guide to real estate investing and dedicated specifically to you. Those that have stood on the sidelines long enough, and now want in! It is a book that speaks directly to the condition of a certain socioeconomic group of people and shows them the way in which they can ameliorate those circumstances, by tapping into the government sponsored Section 8 program.

It is a book that's inclusive of you, and exclusive of others!

You can think of this literary composition in terms of being a picture that best reflects you, your current economic condition, and how you can change it for the better. Here's a question for you. If you are entitled to so much (meaning that, if economic prosperity is yours to have and enjoy), why do you settle for so little? Meditate on that for a moment!

We need to not only get it together my brothers and sisters but once we're established, let's keep it together!

For those of you who purchased this book, and has acknowledged its relevance to your condition, you have a responsibility to tell family members, friends and coworkers about it. I suggest that you coordinate studying time with others that you know purchased the book (in fact, create your own book club on the book's subject matter), so that insightful sharing can take place with one another. Be sure to purchase highlighters for when you come across a text that strikes a chord with you. It is truly time for Us to come together, encourage, educate, and support each other, in our efforts to claim possession of, and socioeconomic control over the communities in which we live.

The time is critical, and the need is pressingly vital for us to also become more politically educated and engaged on the local, state and national level. And this is why, a lot of the political housing decisions that are made at all three different levels, affect the inner-city community properties as a whole, and you, and your family's individual lives as well. The time has come to abandon the misguided practice of seeking to be financially provided for through the employment of others.

Now don't get me wrong. I'm not belittling those that currently are. What I am saying is, "let it just be a steppingstone that propels you to greater heights as real estate Property Equity Niche Investor/ Entrepreneur. "It should be a brief moment in time for you, and not your legacy! Oftentimes in life, we remain stagnant because we view life and its vicissitudes (ups and downs) through someone else's lens. Meaning that we will allow their shortcomings to hinder Us from taking a chance in the area we're interested in venturing into. We never stop to think that maybe the area they decided to get involved with for economic stability just did not jive with their cognitive capabilities.

Which is why they were not successful in the first place.

I have written this book to help you develop (at your own pace) a beginner real estate investment mindset, I have also provided you with a Six step systematic approach to increase the likelihood of success, and I have ultimately made myself available to you (through my direct, one on one consultation services).

There's a Chinese Proverb that says, "A journey of a thousand miles begins with the first step." If you are open minded, this book will educate, illuminate and satiate your appetite to become financially secure! I want to take the time out before I close to express my gratitude to those of you that have supported this writing and applaud your initiative to engage in the process of real estate investing.

Well wishes to you on your journey to economic independence!

Khalfani A. Ajamu

Appendix 1

This is a ____ member partnership between __________, __________, __________, and __________. Designed solely for the purchasing, rehabbing, and the renting out to Section 8 applicants on the respective property located at

____

Building Type (_________)

This partnership agreement with the above-named partners will be in legal force in accordance with the terms set forth in this partnership agreement.

The following named individuals are financial contributors only concerning this venture. And will be responsible for their own tax liability.

Partner's Name________________________________

Said partner will each be required to contribute_______________,

however, the original operating partner will be

____.

I________________, ________________, and ______________,

Have read the above stated partnership provisions and have agreed to it in its entirety.

Partner's Signatures

____

____

____

____

Notary Signature

Appendix 2

3/5/12 How to Apply for Section 8 Housing as a Landlord | eHow.com Page 95

Top 5 To Try

- How to Apply for Section 8 Housing Assistance in Cook County, Illinois
- How to Locate Your Local Housing Authority When You Want to Become a HUD Landlord and Accept Section 8 Vouchers
- How to Apply for Section 8 Housing in Lawrenceburg, Tennessee
- How to Apply for Section 8 Housing in South Carolina
- Applying for Section 8 Housing in Charlotte, NC

How to Apply for Section 8 Housing as a Landlord

By Rocco Pendola, eHow Contributor

The U.S. Department of Housing and Urban Development does not provide the housing stock for the Section 8 program, private property owners do. Section 8 benefits refer to federal subsidies that HUD supplies low-income renters to cover the portion of their market rate rent that exceeds 30 percent to 40 percent of their income. If you own a home, apartment or several units that you would like to rent to Section 8 tenants, you follow the same general process to "apply" across the nation.

Related Searches: FHA Housing Home Care Agency

Difficulty: Moderate

Instructions

1

List your vacancy. You can use traditional sources such as newspapers in addition to advertising your opening at the Go Section 8 website, which specializes in Section 8 listings. Note in your ad that you are willing to accept Section 8 voucher holders.

2

Screen interested applicants. As the Go Section 8 website explains, HUD allows prospective Section 8 landlords to put families using Section 8 assistance through their standard screening process. Follow applicable rental l and do not discriminate and y u can choose between subsidized and u ubsidized renters with no worries.

www.ehow.com/how_7474177_apply-section-8-housing-landlord.html

Page ... E
Page 96

3

Enter a verbal agreement with a Section 8 household you wish to rent to. The Section 8 subsidy holder will give you a packet from the public housing agency that administers the Section 8 program in your area. Complete the Request for Tenancy Approval form and include the other requested documents, which includes an unsigned copy of the lease you intend to sign with the tenant. The renter will forward this information to the public housing agency for review.

4

Schedule an inspection when the agency [illegible] you. Before you can formalize an [illegible]m[illegible]nt [illegible] a Section 8 family, the agency in[illegible]cts your property to ensure it meets HUD's Housing Quality Standards. Broadly speaking, you must provide a safe and sanitary environment for your tenants, which includes safe and working electrical, plumbing, heating and waste management systems. If your unit fails part of the inspection, your public housing agency will give you ample time to rectify the situation.

5

Sign a one-year lease with the Section 8 family after the public housing agency approves your unit. HUD requires all initial Section 8 agreements be one-year [illegible]. Execute a Housing Assistance Paym[illegible] contract with the public housing agency. This pact outlines the responsibilities of the landlord, tenant and the a[illegible]ncy un[illegible]er [illegible] Section 8 arrangement.

Tips & Warnings

Your public housing agency reinspects your unit annually to verify that it continues to meet HUD's standards.

I Need Information on Becoming a Section 8 Landlord

By Jackie Lohrey, eHow Contributor | updated March 13, 2011

Section 8, also called the Housing Choice Voucher Program, is a rental subsidy program for low-income, elderly and disabled persons. Although the U.S. Department of Housing and Urban Development funds Section 8, local public housing agencies are responsible for administering the program and monitoring rental properties. So, getting the information you need to become a Section 8 landlord starts with contacting your local public housing agency.

Related Searches: Low Income Housing Rental Agency

Identification

Not every community participates in the Section 8 program so your first step is to verify program participation with your local housing authority or check with HUD via its website. Once you verify that your community participates, inform your local public housing agency that you want to be on the Section 8 housing list. Listing your property is free and once you do, no further action is necessary until you find and start the process of approving a Section 8 tenant. You can also include a statement in any rental advertisements that you accept Section 8 vouchers.

The Facts

Property safety and maintenance is a major

Page 98 E

Section 8 concern. Although being a Section 8 landlord is, in many respects, no different than any other landlord-tenant situation, you will be subject to an extensive property inspection before your tenant moves in and then annually as long as your tenant remains in the unit. If you fail any part of the home inspection, all repairs must be complete before your tenant can move in or within the time an inspector gives you if your tenant is already in the unit. If you want to conduct your own inspection for assessment purposes, ask your local public housing agency for a copy of the inspection form or download a copy at the HUD website.

Process

Becomin | a Section 8 landlord means, in some cases, modifying your monthly rental charge. The total out-of-pocket rental expense your tenant pays each month must be at least 30 percent but cannot exceed 40 percent of his adjusted gross income, according to HUD. For example, if the normal rent for a unit is $1,200 per month and you receive 70 percent, or $840 in the form of a Section 8 voucher, this leaves the tenant responsible for the remaining $360. If this amount is more than 40 percent of the tenant's adjusted gross income, you will need to lower the monthly rent to comply.

Paperwork

The process you follow when screening prospective tenants, signing and enforcing terms of a lease, and collecting the portion of the monthly rent for which your tenant is responsible includes additional paperwork. Your prospective tenant will first present a Request for Tenancy Approval form at the time you approve the rental application. Your signature and information you provide is necessary to schedule the property inspection. After the inspection is complete, you sign a contract with the housing authority and include a Section 8 addendum to the lease your tenant signs.

Page 99 Exhib D

Top 5 To Try

I Need Information on Becoming a Section 8 Landlord

HUD Requirements for Landlords

The Downside for Landlords Accepting Section 8

How to Become a Section 8 Landlord

Section 8 Housing Requirements for Landlords

Landlord Requirements for Section 8 Rentals

By Cynthia Clark, eHow Contributor

Section 8 is a federal program that provides subsidized rent payments to landlords on behalf of qualifying individuals. The U.S. Department of Housing and Urban Development (HUD) manages the program through state and county authorities. Individuals qualify for the program and look for homes or apartments from landlords willing to abide by HUD requirements for rentals.

Related Searches: Rent Furnished Apartment New Housing

Screen Potential Tenants

Landlords are responsible for screening potential tenants. HUD qualifies individuals for the subsidized rent program based upon family size and income. Landlords may screen tenants as they would non-Section 8 tenants by taking applications and performing background and credit checks.

Provide a HUD Approved Lease

One of the requirements of a Section 8 landlord is to provide a lease to the tenant that meets HUD requirements and clearly outlines what is expected from both the tenant and the landlord.

Receive Deposits and Rents

Upon acceptance of a lease, the landlord will collect deposits and reduced rents directly from the tenant. Rents and deposits are held by the landlord as they would in any other situation not subsidized by Section 8. The subsidized portion of the rent will be mailed to the landlord from HUD at the first of every month.

Property Maintenance

HUD cites that the landlord must "provide decent, safe, and sanitary housing to a tenant at a reasonable rent." The apartment

Page 100

or home must pass inspection and be maintained to basic requirements for decent living as long as Section 8 payments are being received. The inspector will evaluate the exterior and every room of the rental for basic standards of cleanliness and safety. If utilities are provided by the landlord, they must be turned on. If a stove and refrigerator are provided by the landlord, those appliances are also subject to inspection.

Provide Services Outlined in Lease

If rent includes utilities or trash pick-up, the landlord is responsible for paying for those services. If there are common areas or yards of apartment buildings, the landlord is responsible for lighting, cleaning and maintenance of those areas.

Enforce Property Rules

To maintain a property that provides a quality of life to all tenants and neighbors, landlords must enforce rules and regulations regarding noise, cleanliness and crime deterrents. If necessary, contact law enforcement authorities regarding criminal activity.

Related Searches

Low Income Housing

Landlord Lease

Landlord Tenant Lease

Apartments for Rent

Temporary Housing

References

HUD: Housing Choice Vouchers Fact Sheet

HUD: Inspection Form for Rental Units

Resources

 Page 101 Exhibi D

Top 5 To Try

- The Downside for Landlords Accepting Section 8
- Section 8 Rent Guidelines
- Landlords and Section 8
- How to Rent to Section 8 Voucher Recipients
- How Much Over the Section 8 Standard Can a Landlord Raise the Rent?

Section 8 Rent Guidelines for Landlords

By Robert Rimm, eHow Contributor

The housing allowance program run by the federal government, known as Section 8, delivers rent subsidies for low-income families through certificates and vouchers. It is a component of the Housing and Community Development Act from 1974, written to make safe and clean housing accessible to families with limited means, rented from private landlords.

Related Searches: For Rent Properties to Rent

Rental Payments

Households must meet strict eligibility standards, after which they are entitled to participate in the Section 8 program. They are typically required to pay a maximum of 30 percent of monthly income for rent and utilities. The program then pays the rest of the approval rental amount directly to the private landlord, who must maintain the property and provide all reasonable repairs.

Rental Amounts and Increases

The property's owner is responsible for establishing the rental amounts for each unit according to U.S. Department of Housing and Urban Development standards of "rent reasonableness." Local housing authorities look at similar rents in a given neighborhood to ensure that landlords do not charge excessive amounts, as the housing authority must approve all Section 8 contracts. The property owners can ask for rental increases, subject to local guidelines and supporting documents.

Tenant Screenings

Both landlords and the local housing authority that administers the Section 8 plan are responsible for screening tenants. Once the authority approves prospective tenants

Page 102

based on need, income and other predetermined criteria, as well as a background check for all adult participants, the landlord then takes over the process to approve suitable tenants, including ensuring that a given unit does not house more tenants than legally permitted.

Evictions

As with private tenants, landlords can begin nonpayment proceedings against any Section 8 tenant who violates the lease's terms for payment or other items. All such circumstances must adhere to local, state and federal law. Property owners must adhere to further procedures according to the requirements of Section 8 provisions, provide additional forms and await housing authority approval before commencing any eviction action.

Related Searches

Low Income Housing

For Rent by Owner

New Housing

Help Pay Rent

FHA Housing

References

U.S. Department of Housing and Urban Development: Section 8 Program Background Information

MassResources.org: Landlord's Guide to Section 8

Resources

New York City Housing Authority: Section 8 Assistance

You May Also Like

Section 8 Rent Guidelines

172

www.ingramcontent.com/pod-product-compliance
Lightning Source LLC
LaVergne TN
LVHW020414220926
848484LV00018B/2574/J
* 9 7 9 8 2 1 8 1 3 2 6 6 8 *